# PIECES OF EIGHT

Noah Webster says in his book that Pieces of Eight are "the obsolete Spanish and Spanish American dollar, equal to eight Reals." One must now look up Reals. But instead, I have decided just to borrow the mystery and romance of these words and use them for the title of my memoirs.

\*\*\*\*\*\*

Said the alchemist, when old,
"Only memories turn to gold."

\*\*\*\*\*\*

This work would not have been possible without a generous grant which provided sustenance and encouragement from Sarah Taylor Morrison.

\*

Thanks are also due to Joe Medlicott for the original inspiration and to Philip Reynolds for unrelenting (!) editing.

# Pieces of Eight

Walter N. Morrison

This book is set in Garamond Premier Pro and Lucida Calligraphy typefaces.

Layout & production: Michael Morrison, digital-illuminations.com.
Original cover painting: Chloe Kettlewell.
Printing & publication: Lulu.com.

ISBN-13: 978-1-4357-0489-3

# PREFACE

After running for 73 years I had made it to the end of the century, 2000, with a pretty strong finish. Now, however, my knees said skiing, mountain climbing and working on my farm were no longer my future. What would I do on Monday mornings the rest of my life? On Tuesday afternoons? There was a long way to go. I needed a desk job. Could I face it? Thus I was ready to look, to consider, when chance brought me the news of a course in memoir writing taught at The Institute for Lifelong Education at Dartmouth, ILEAD. The rest is history, *Pieces of Eight*.

I had never written anything much except business letters, and only in the most gingerly fashion had I ever thought about trying more,---to be a writer. I suspect that the immense challenge presented, and fear of failure, had prevented me from admitting what was actually the truth, that I wanted to write. So I confessed it. Then, should I take this course? It was important for me that men of my age and background had praised the course and its teacher, but what finally determined me to apply was the news that I might not be able to get enrolled. The course had been oversubscribed for many years. Suddenly I knew it was a good program and I had to get accepted. And luckily, by lot, I was.

We were required to submit a first memoir before classes began. With great enthusiasm I wrote (an early version of) *How It Started,* and turned it in. The story was about a **unique** man and my **unique** relationship with him starting when I was twelve. It was also full of wonderful long forgotten information about skiing in the 1930s, colorful digressions about 1936 Ford station wagons---blue ones to be exact---and complete details about how I made my own first pair of ski bindings. I already felt that being a writer was wonderful. Why had I not done this before? I couldn't wait for the accolades of the class.

Professor Joe Medlicott, 82nd Airborne June 1944, Deerfield Academy, University of Conn, and now Dartmouth, moved slowly around the classroom table returning our papers. Even before he handed it to me I could see on my paper more of his blue pencil than my black ink. How could he? I was suddenly wiped out with apprehension and embarrassment. He stood by me with the pages of my story bending forward out over his hand where not only I but the whole class could see the vast glaring blue of the editing pencil. He was actually speaking, but I did not hear a word of what he said. "When a Mafia hit man finally finds his man he points the pistol carefully at the victim's head, and then before pulling the trigger he says, 'You know, there ain't nothing poisonal about this.' BANG. Well, class, that's the way I want you to take my editing. Nothing personal."

Nothing personal! Ha! To save my ego I was quickly turning my disappointment and embarrassment into outrage. How could he refer to my most treasured and totally unique memory as the "standard boy finds mentor story", how could he say my artful digressions were irrelevant distractions, and above all how could he say I must cut the whole thing down, my freshly created virgin writing, by two thirds. He could as well ask me to abandon two of my three sons. I decided to fight. So we did fight, for about three classes, but he won. The Paratrooper was an expert in this fight, the Marine was not. My next story, *Souvenir*, was so short and skeletal most of the class wanted it longer. But I didn't.

In *Pieces of Eight* I am trying to remember and write the truth. These are memoirs. But they are written as stories, and in order to shape an historical recounting of events into the formed structure and sequence that we enjoy as a story the pen must occasionally be dipped into that proverbial ink of poetic license. I have dipped. Events, though real, have been moved in time and/or space. As an example, important to Marines, I was screened for Officer Candidate School in both Parris Island in 1945 and Quantico in 1951 but gather all events together in Quantico 1951. In the interests of privacy the names in some stories have been changed. But I notice, without exact measurement, that my small bottle of this useful ink is still well more than half full.

Novels carefully work through plot and develop character. In contrast, the essence of the short story, critics say, is discovery. In memoir-short stories the discovery is usually about oneself. And whether a goal or not, writing such stories is most certainly self-discovery. I learned more about my feelings for my father in writing *Souvenir* than I had learned in 70 previous years of life. Better late than never. *Pieces of Eight* will be a success if you enjoy discovering some of its discoveries. I hope you do.

Walter N. Morrison
Truro 2007

# PIECES OF EIGHT

# SOUVENIR

It was a small leather-covered box, old and dried out and turning tan where it had probably once been a richer brown. Gold embossing on the edges was faded and had worn off in some places. But it fit nicely in my hand and felt as though it belonged there. There were brass hinges on the back and a pressure clamp on the front. After years of sealed darkness it opened easily and quickly. The lining inside was loose, plumped up, watered silk, rather like a miniature coffin.

I found this box in the back drawer of my father's desk ten years after his death. Only after my mother died had I faced the job of going through all their things and cleaning up their house of many years.

My father had grown up on a California ranch where he had learned to ride and shoot. At college he had been a good student, but his real talent and only outstanding activity was riflery. In my favorite picture of him he sits on a fence with his teammates and their rifles beside them. A sign says "Intercollegiate Champions 1911". He was Captain of the team.

In 1918 he went to war in France as an army private. He was in or near some of the big battles of that year, battles I don't know the names of because I don't think he ever told me. Once he said that he was positioned along side some Marines and that they were a "crack" unit. I used to think that maybe the reason he never said much about the war was because he was a private, not an officer, and that his brothers and friends had all fought as officers. I don't think he often felt proud of himself. But there can be other reasons veterans don't talk much.

If he did not volunteer such things and I did not ask, nonetheless I think he was a good father for me. He was not close, and not warm, and perhaps not what we now call supportive, but we met on intellectual grounds: geology, history, investments. Further, although I was only a mildly interested student, he taught me to shoot and I, too, became an expert.

But as I opened this old, cracked leather box from his desk, it took me a few moments to begin to realize what was in it. Anyone who has sorted through the belongings of a dead parent knows the strange, even frightening, feelings of sadness and excitement as old photos are uncurled and studied, letters cautiously read, and the miscellaneous ephemera of theatre tickets, invitations, awards and citations are studied for clues to the now dead parent's long, private and sometimes secret life. What I saw was an oval metal disc about 2 1/2 inches long, either zinc or hardened lead, slightly corroded but with a still visible name and some numbers and unfamiliar markings stamped on it. I lifted it out of the box and turned it over. There was something on the back. Stuck there with dried-out adhesive tape were service ribbons, military service ribbons. They came off easily and I quickly recognized them as US ribbons, some of which I knew. The World War 1 Victory Ribbon, the Rainbow Division ribbon. There were others which I thought to be battle or campaign ribbons, three with stars. These were my father's. Slowly, and with images of my father in uniform beginning to flood my mind, I turned the metal disc back over again and carefully read the name on it: ANTON ACKERMANN, OBERFELL-KRS-GOAR. 24 II 93. Beneath this were the numbers of a Battalion and a Division and a serial number. This was a German soldier's dog tag. My father had attached with tape his own service ribbons to the dog tag of a German soldier and placed them together in this leather box for somebody to find. For me.

Over time I have thought of many stories. Anton Ackermann was a young German infantry man. Just the sound of his name makes me think of loving parents picking it carefully. He was killed in battle and then found dead by my father who, on the move, stopped just long enough to take the dog tag as a souvenir.

I haven't liked this story. A better one has my father and his buddies, while digging in for the night in a forest, discover a nearby corpse. They bury Anton in some decent way, and feel justified or even respectful in removing and saving the dog tag.

Occasionally, moved by a different and strong need and emotion in me, I picture my father as the man in his platoon who spots the German in a tree. He is a sniper who has been skillfully picking off American soldiers. My father takes his own slow and careful aim and with one shot kills him. Anton drops to the ground dead. My father takes the dog tag. He thinks about Anton all his life and finally puts his own service ribbons joined together in the box with Anton's tag.

# HOW IT STARTED

In a school yard on a cold snowy Saturday morning in December 1939 I met a man who taught me, in time, how to ski and climb mountains, how to paddle a canoe and catch trout. But on just the first day we met I learned even more; it could be fun to be helpful, an idea that, when it came, jumped into an empty space in my head, a space that seemed just shaped for it, ready and waiting, now that I was twelve.

A friend from a private school, Kingswood, had invited me to go on a ski trip with one of his teachers. I had never been to Kingswood and was apprehensive about it — at the time I might have used the word scared rather than apprehensive, but of course I wouldn't have actually said either. As we gathered at the school I didn't know any of the boys jumping out of their parents big cars. They were all yelling out to each other and throwing their skis and poles—the ones with those big old 8 inch baskets on them—helter skelter onto the back of the lowered wooden tailgate of an old blue Ford station wagon. I stood there and watched. After all the gear had been thrown in and the boys had fought over the seats in the car, Mr. James Goodwin came around to close the tailgate where I was standing alone. He said something nice to me right away and said I must be Jack Lee's friend. I could tell that he was glad the parents had left and we were alone now. He tried to close the tailgate, but I had figured it wouldn't work because the skis were sticking out too far. He had been too busy with the parents to make sure the boys had loaded their skis in far enough. He pushed hard on the skis and tried to raise the tailgate. It wouldn't close. He had to lower it again, and push harder, and juggle the skis in further before he could finally get it to shut. I watched, but I didn't help. Then this teacher, Mr. Goodwin, with quick intuition, or maybe careful planning, moved his Adirondack pack basket from the middle of the front seat to the way back of the car and asked me to sit next to him. Jack was next to me by the front window.

This was at the end of the Great Depression, a period that had been difficult and discouraging for my father. My family did not have as much money as most of their friends, but my father now had an office job that was steady, and most important, for me, he now had been able to buy me a new pair of skis and boots. I loved skiing almost as much as bike riding, fishing, and running model airplane motors. And it was in fact my father who first took me skiing. He had brought our family East in 1927 just after I was born. His health had given out and he could no longer work in the gold and silver mines of Grass Valley, California and Park City, Utah. Skis came with us on that move. During the winter months miners in those mountains would "ski" in their free time. The sport consisted in going straight downhill as fast and as far as they could in the deep unpacked powder. I don't know whether my Dad was any good at it or not. I hadn't been old enough to see him do it, but at least he brought the skis east with us. They were made of wood, the smallest of the three pairs was about 6 feet long and almost too heavy for me to carry. If there had also been poles, which miners didn't use, I couldn't have carried them.

My first ski trip had been using these skis when I was 7 or 8 years old. The whole family had walked to a little park close to home in West Hartford. We all bravely tried to make a straight run down the gentle slope without falling, but large clumps of field grass and brush sticking up through the thin snow made it impossible to steer or control these old board skis with their

loose leather toe straps. My father was unable to show us what
his skill had been in the deep powder of the western mountains,
the country that he came from and still loved and missed. I
think he was sad. In turn we each fell down on every attempted
run. My sister was very cold and unhappy. We were going back
up the hill to go home when I decided to try one more time.
Slowly, determined, and with arms flailing through the air, I did
succeed in a full run to the bottom of the slope. But when I
looked back hopefully to see if they had been watching my family was just disappearing over the top of the hill and I had to run
to catch up. However, that day, still vivid in my memory, was
when my love of skiing was born. Unfortunately, it was the only
time I ever skied with my father, though I don't entirely know
why that was the case. I don't think he skied again in all his life.
But at least I can say he started me. I owe him for that. I wish it
had been more.

Our Kingswood trip was headed for Norfolk where the golf
course was an early Connecticut ski mecca. Our route led over
Avon Mountain which was then the known limit of my ex-
plored 12 year old's world and even the direction was exciting,
Northwest. That was the land of lumberjacks, wild animals,
hunting, fishing, and adventure. My discomfort at being the
outsider in the group was now also being made easier by friendly
Mr. Goodwin. He wasn't a kid like us, but he was still young,
wasn't very big, and acted as though he might be a little uncomfortable himself, or at least knew what it felt like to be an outsider. Maybe he too, I thought, had sometimes found it hard to
fit in with a band of loud, rowdy jocks.

After that first experience with my family I had skied a few
times every winter on the little hills around the neighborhood
and parks in West Hartford. For the most part we kids taught
ourselves how to ski, but I remember an Austrian woman, an
escapee from the Germans (which to us boys gave her mystery
and authority) who tried to teach us how to do telemark turns

with just our toe strap bindings. I can still hear her heavily accented voice crying out the classic "bend zee knees."

Soon the first modern bindings showed up in our sports store and I studied them all with an interest not always shown in school classes. I even tried to make a pair. Eventually, perhaps a year or so before this, my first big first ski trip to Norfolk, my parents had bought me a new pair of hickory ridge-top skis, real ski boots meant just for skiing, and Dovre bear trap bindings. So I approached this big day able to make a good snowplow turn and able to climb back uphill with a rough herringbone technique. But I was worried about how much better than I these private school boys might be able to ski.

It didn't take too long to find out. Jack Lee, my friend, was about the best skier of us all and I was pretty good. The golf course was, by any modern standard, pretty limited and tame. But there was one high knoll with a golf tee on top and a fairway stretching gently downhill for some distance to the North. On the slope there were several groves of pine trees and some sand traps that when covered with snow gave boys just what boys are always looking for in a ski hill, jumps.

We skied down and herringboned back up the same little runs over and over again. We raced each other. We fell down a lot, some more than others. We found the jumps and leapt off them, taking turns marking for each other how far we had flown through the air. Nobody told us to be careful. First by accident and then on purpose we went sailing through the pine groves knocking down our backs the loads of snow from the heavily laden boughs. Clumps of snow balled up on our prickly woolen winter clothes. Mr. Goodwin told everybody how good their skiing was. He said things like "Gee Whizzikers" and "Jim Dandy". Bindings came off or broke. When the kids couldn't fix them Mr. Goodwin tried to, his bare fingers in the cold snow, using a bent screw driver and a pair of rusty pliers.

One of the boys had the newest type of binding, called a Ski-Free, and nobody knew how to adjust it when it came loose. Everybody started arguing about it. I'd seen it in the sports store and knew what to do. I started to tell Mr. Goodwin but he just handed me the pliers and screw driver and told me I could probably do it better than he could. "Go to it," he said. I could tell he really meant it. So I unscrewed the top plate, put the little ball bearing back in its groove where it belonged and tightened the top back down. Mr. Goodwin had a big smile and said, "By golly, I thought you could," and somebody else said, "Neat". A boy called Chester said, "I told you that's how." Everybody else said, "Yeah, in a pigs ear you did."

We ate lunch from our packs on top of the high tee. The sandwiches were stiff and cold, the chocolate bars were hard and snapped when you bit off a piece and the apples were frozen almost solid. Mr. Goodwin sat and talked with us just about the way we did ourselves. He gave his sandwich to a boy whose mother had not packed him much lunch. Mr. Goodwin said he wasn't hungry, but I wasn't sure it was true. He was different.

Later in the afternoon he led us to another spot on the golf course where there was a short, steep slope. We all practiced making parallel or "Christie" turns, hard for kids to learn with the stiff high camber skis of the time. But Mr. Goodwin did the turns with us over and over again. We all fell a lot. Finally, when it was getting late and cold, Chester fell hard with a bad twist to his leg. His knee hurt and started to swell so we headed back to the station wagon.

Everybody was cold and tired. It was beginning to get dark. Mr. Goodwin had the tailgate down and this time was trying to pack the skis in far enough when Chester, now in the car with his knee braced up, called out that he had left his lunch knapsack up on the high tee. I saw Mr. Goodwin's face. There was a look, not much, but not happy. I felt I was the only one who saw it. He didn't say anything. Then suddenly out of my mouth

9

jumped the words "I'll get it." And at that moment it started. A new desire and a strong and happy new emotion for a boy. I wanted to help. To help without being asked. I wanted to help this man. He said I didn't need to, he'd go get it. But I did need to. With my skis on, I was quickly up the hill, herring-boning, and back down with the pack, feeling weightless all the way, and did a Christie at the bottom right by the car. He was alone there, still standing outside by the tailgate, waiting in the cold and said, "Holy Smokes, that was terrific."

He's still saying it, 68 years later, and I'm still hearing it. Probably always will.

# THE MAHOOSUCS

At fifteen years old and dead tired from a long day's hike, we were sleeping so soundly that we did not hear them before they stepped on our legs and put their busy hands on us through our thin sleeping bags. We awoke together, startled, frightened. It was totally dark and even toward the front opening of the lean-to, toward our feet, nothing could be seen, not even a silhouette of a shape against the mountain sky. "Who are they?" I choked out a whisper toward Jack. "I don't know," came back an answer with plaintiveness and fear. Suddenly Jack's pack basket on the log at the front of the lean-to was thrown over on us and then, while we curled up to protect ourselves, they banged the tin frying pan against the cooking pot at the fireplace.

Since dusk, alone on our first night on this faraway hiking trip, apprehension and uneasiness, though unspoken, had been quietly growing in us. Our parents were right, we were not yet old enough to be here alone. At the banging of the frying pan we screamed. In the dark, surrounded and attacked by the primordial monsters of all childhoods, we screamed. And we screamed the scream of children, but it was for only a moment and for the last time. Emboldened by our own volume and power, the screams turned into yells. We weren't children, and there were two of us. We jumped up and yelled louder. We were already discovered, we would yell as loud as we could. We did. All around us there was a rushing and rustling noise as they, many of them, retreated into the woods in all directions and left us suddenly in silence.

We were pretty sure now they weren't people, but we didn't know what it was out there, waiting for us, ringing our camp in the pitch-dark woods. Get a flashlight. We shone it at the edge of the woods, moving the beam slowly along, and there, as bright and smiley as daylight, was a friendly face looking back at us. A raccoon. There were more, waiting patiently at the edge of the clearing, waiting, it seemed, to be invited in, or at least waiting for us to go back to sleep so they could return to their ravages and revels. We laughed, the loose, shaky laugh of released emotion, and quickly became happy with our adventure.

"At first I thought it was you grabbing my legs," said Jack.

"Yeah, same here, but I knew you weren't out there throwing the pack basket at us, so it had to be somebody else. Christ, I was scared. I saw a raccoon once but I never knew they came around like this at night."

"Look at this," said Jack, shining the light at our pile of equipment and food beside the fireplace. A dozen eggs which the man at the grocery store had put in an extra strong carton for us were now a neat row of empty shells. At first we were more amazed than concerned, but then we saw the bread, or what was left of it.

"It looks like they got most of one loaf and part of the other one, too. What are we going to eat the peanut butter and jelly on?"

"On Hydrox cookies, on sardines, on our fingers, I guess. Christ, I hope we have enough left to eat."

We needed food for three more days and two more nights, maybe three more nights, depending on how many miles we could travel each day. We would find out.

The Mahoosuc Range, with fifteen summits between 3000 and 4000 feet, stretches and zigzags between Gorham, New Hampshire, and Grafton Notch, Maine, without much in the way of civilization for many miles on either side. The Appalachian Trail, on its way from Georgia to Mount Katahdin, runs along this ridge for about thirty miles and traverses many of the high peaks including Old Speck, the highest of all, at the northern end of the range. Old Speck, if we could get to it, was higher than any other mountain in Maine, except Katahdin. 4180 feet. We kept thinking about that.

Jack Lee and I had been sent off to our first year of prep school together and this was now our first summer vacation. Neither of us had wanted to go to a summer camp, something that had been offered to us, and what many of our friends were doing. But neither of us were joiners and what we both really wanted was a job and independence. The times, wartime, favored such boys because grown manpower was in short supply. Up until the time of this trip in August, Jack had been working at Tatro's farm in Farmington. Tatro had sheep and milking cattle and Jack helped out in general but shoveled a lot of manure in particular. I had a better job. The Alling Rubber Company was Hartford's biggest sporting-goods store and had a small branch store in West Hartford where I lived. The store stocked everything I was interested in; fishing tackle, sneakers, bathing suits, basketballs, .22 caliber rifles and ammunition, skis and bicycles. I was the only employee and soon learned to know the stock better than the manager, who was a nice guy, ate baked bean sandwiches, and had a girlfriend somewhere. I ended up running the store, quite often alone. When stock ran low I called the Hartford store and told Mr. Alling what we needed. He showed up one day and asked me where Mr. Morrison was. When he found out he closed the store, put me in his big Buick and drove me to an office in Hartford where I was issued my Social Security card. The clerk said they had never before given a card to anyone under sixteen. Mr. Alling shook my hand and said, "Congratulations, Mr. Morrison, and welcome to the staff of Alling Rubber."

Jack and I had gotten to Gorham, the starting point of our trip, by train. We left from Hartford and were pulled all day by old coal-fired steam locomotives. We changed at Springfield, continued up the Connecticut River Valley, changed again at White River Junction, and then proceeded on to Gorham. Near Gorham Jack's grandmother lived at her huge estate, The Rocks, and we stayed with her for a night. Our visit to the grandmother may have helped Jack's parents feel we would be safe, as if the old lady could rescue us if we had cut a vein with the firewood ax. As for my parents, I can only credit them for being brave to let me go. As boys, we could see no possible reason why we shouldn't go and were probably rather hard to reason with.

The Gorham IGA had a full selection of what hikers ate in those days which was exactly the same food everybody else ate. No dehydrated food, just cans of Spam, corned beef hash, and baked beans. Also they had cans of Vegall, which Jimmy Goodwin always made us eat on his trips so that he could look our parents in the eye and say we ate well. Making our own decisions at last, we skipped the Vegall. The only dessert we knew about was fruit cocktail in heavy sugar syrup. It came in just the right size can for two boys to share. But a single can of Spam, hash, or beans was definitely not enough to give each of us a full meal, but two cans of each were too heavy. We needed it but couldn't carry it. We finally chose just four cans, one for each night at each of the lean-tos positioned at roughly even distances along the trail. This was an early experience in no-win situations. We had probably made the right decision, but it was the hungry decision. Lunch was always sardines and peanut butter and jelly in large quantities on a couple pieces of squashed bread. For breakfast we took oranges but skipped the usual Goodwin oatmeal, not focusing on its virtue of being raccoon safe. Instead we went for luxury, fried eggs and two pounds of bacon. Finally, Hydrox cookies in quantity for Jack and Baby Ruth bars for me.

We drank water from all brooks in those days, unless we saw a cow actually peeing immediately upstream.

Jack had a good pack basket, and I had a totally inadequate canvas Boy Scout knapsack. By the time everything was loaded in, with homemade sleeping bags of sewn blankets rolled on top, a frying pan and pot with Jack and an old, lightweight Collins canoe ax hanging off my back we were heavily laden. The guys in the store were all for us, wishing us well, giving us extra matches in a wet-proof can, and finally getting us a ride down to the bridge over the Androscoggin River where the Appalachian Trail begins its ascent to the Mahoosuc Range.

Cascade Mountain, Trident Col, Wocket Ledge, Bald Cap, Dream Lake, Dryad Falls, and Gentian Pond, with its lean-to shelter for our first night. These names had music and mystery, they were northern, spoke of wildness, of hunters, loggers, and animals. We weren't just reading another story in our favorite magazine, "Boy's Life", we were ourselves right where adventures happened. So we climbed. We climbed altogether about three thousand feet up and about one thousand feet down and covered the ten miles to the lean-to just in time to set up camp and eat supper before dark. The day, the longest of the trip, had in fact been difficult and the packs were too heavy, especially the canned goods poking into my thinly padded ribs, but we had made it and felt newly confident. If at dusk and in the darkness following we felt some kind of loneliness, we had, after all, met not a single person all day nor seen any signs of recent use along the trail. We knew that to feel this slightly scary way must be part of being in the wilderness. We were glad to be there together. We went to sleep.

Since that night, the night of raccoons at Gentian Pond, I don't think either of us has ever been afraid of the dark again. If this was the positive side of the experience, at breakfast a more thorough assessment of our reduced food supply warned of possible negative consequences. There were only seven pieces of bread left unravished, although there were a lot of raccoon-mouthed crusts and crumbs. They had eaten the dozen eggs on the spot, but after sampling one Baby Ruth bar and leaving the wrapper they had apparently taken all the rest away with them. This was confirmation of the fact that Baby Ruth bars were better than Hydrox cookies, a very important matter between us, but on the other hand I was hoping that Jack would, surely, let me have a few of his cherished Hydrox. As we sopped up the bacon grease with the raccoon crusts, the hot grease killing any germs, we decided that we would really have to make a major effort to do the trip in just two more nights instead of three more. We had brought only minimal food to begin with because of the weight, with nobody to carry it but ourselves, and now it was clear that we did not have enough to keep us going for three more nights.

In the morning, our packs were actually a few pounds lighter, but, as packs do on the second day, they felt heavier and our feet were sore. But the thought of scaling the next big peak, Mount Success, and then Goose Eye Mountain if we could in fact go fast enough to skip the lean-to in between, drew us on. You couldn't fail with a mountain called Success and we didn't. We were hungry, however, and our lunch, with one piece of bread each for our peanut butter and jelly, didn't fill us up. And by the time we descended from Mount Success and traversed several smaller peaks, we knew we didn't have the power to try for Goose Eye. In late afternoon at the Carlo Col Shelter we split the can of Spam and the second fruit cocktail, sat around the fire for a while, and went to bed. We slept with the remaining bread and other raccoon edibles in our sleeping bags with us. Tomorrow we would try again to double up the miles.

But it didn't happen. Even though our packs finally felt lighter,—well more than half the food was gone thanks to help from the raccoons—and we were not as stiff and sore on this third day, we soon realized we would not get over four peaks and pass through famous Mahoosuc Notch to spend the night at the last shelter, Speck Pond, all on this one day. It would, we had to recognize, end up being four nights and five days done on about three days food. We became philosophical and humorous despite the hunger, fatigue, and sore feet.

Help with the humor came in a surprising discovery; we were not alone on this trail after all. There were footprints, fresh ones, in the little flat damp places on the trail, going the same direction we were, toward Old Speck. We had not seen them before, and it had not rained, so it was a mystery how they suddenly came there before us. We studied them intently for clues and found it curious that they were made by a shoe with crepe rubber soles. Crepe rubber was the latest new shoe fashion in 1942, and we immediately began to fantasize about what kind of person was leading us on. Probably because we were now continually thinking about food we named him "Mr. Crepe Suzette." Neither of us had ever had a Crepe Suzette or even really knew what one was, but we knew they were very good to eat, so every time we saw his footprint we called out "Crepe Suzette."

But by the end of the next afternoon, as we approached our last lean-to, Speck Pond, our energies and our spirits were just about exhausted. Jack's sneakers, high tops, were old ones and the soles had now almost completely separated from the canvas uppers. Rubber was not as good during wartime, and sneakers then were never as substantially made as they are now. But Jack, showing early on his thoughtfulness about tools, spare parts, and equipment, had brought along a roll of black cloth electrical tape, precursor of duct tape. He wrapped both feet completely around with the tape and thus was able to keep the soles under his feet, most of the time, if he stepped carefully. Crepe Suzette was still tantalizingly ahead of us, but now our gut feelings were more powerfully affected by the knowledge that all we had left for supper was just one, too-small, can of hash and a few Hydrox cookies, not even a fruit cocktail.

However, just as such things should happen, lying in wait for us around the last curve of trail before the Lean-to we found beauty, poetry, and nourishment, and all in sufficient amounts to make our last night the best. Speck Pond rests on the precariously narrow high shoulder of Old Speck Mountain, held from cascading off into space by fringes of hemlock and balsam fir with their thin, northern, spiring tops. As we turned the corner it lay before us, black waters deathly still, telling of depth, and the peak itself rising six hundred feet above it in the background. On that shore, beneath the peak, in a little clearing from which the firs had receded, someone, it seemed, had painted a picture of the perfect camping lean-to, low-slung large old logs and graceful roof of moss-covered shingles, facing us across the water. A thin curl of smoke rose from the fireplace.

"Wow! what a pretty place," I said. We just stood and looked for a few moments. Then Jack, showing his Andover education said, "You know what this is, it's a tarn. That's what you call a small lake in the mountains, a tarn."

"You mean like the one in that poem we had to study in English class?"

"Yeah. By Edgar Allen Poe," Jack said. "But I can't remember exactly how it goes."

"There's supposed to be somebody dying, or drowning, to make it a tarn, I think."

"Well, I can't remember, but you know what, I think maybe Crepe Suzette is there with that fire."

While we were thinking about this and still gazing at the scene, the much needed nourishment of a second course to our dinner miraculously arrived before us. Stepping slowly out of the woods at the side of the trail about thirty feet ahead of us a large fat grouse presented itself, breast forward and now standing stock still. In one smooth motion I picked up a stone and threw it straight for the bird, hitting it dead center in the chest. It collapsed, we rushed forward in amazed excitement, and in a moment were holding a feast triumphantly overhead. Old photos of playing baseball show me as the pitcher and Jack the catcher, but I had never thrown like this before, nor ever since.

Crepe Suzette had again eluded us, slipping on ahead perhaps to spend the night on the top of Old Speck. We kicked his fire to life, plucked the bird and roasted it on a green stick over the flames. Hash and grouse, perfect, and we were nearly full. Dusk was still lonely, but maybe not scary.

On the last morning, with absolutely nothing for breakfast but bacon, we decided that Jimmy Goodwin had thought as wisely about bacon as he had about many other important things. It was dumb to carry the weight of bacon for twenty or thirty miles, then cook it and throw the grease away. We had been trying to eat the grease, but without bread to sop it up, it was more than we could do to just take a spoon and eat it. The answer was, according to Jimmy, to cook bacon only very slightly. We did this, and the fat must have provided the energy that got us over Old Speck that last day, but we had the impression that we were eating small, warm eels. I still can't throw bacon grease away without thinking about this.

Old Speck did turn out to be a snap, and we sat triumphantly on our first summit over four thousand feet. Crepe Suzette had disappeared again and we had eaten our last food, but we knew that our hiking from here on was all downhill to paved Route 26 which led to Bethel, a diner where we could get something to eat, and to the train. Descending became genuinely painful for Jack, as the tape had finally worn through and left his soles to flop off to either side. He walked essentially barefoot down the very long last rocky trail. We had expected to get a ride promptly; in those days everybody picked everybody up, and in truth the first vehicle that came along did stop for us. But if drivers were friendly and helpful, their gasoline was rationed and they came by only rarely. We had walked an hour down the road, a major state highway, toward Bethel before the farmer in the hay truck came along and gave us the lift. He dropped us at the train station, where we left our packs, and told us where we could find refreshments.

Walking up the main street of town to Klueckey's Drug Store, I gave Jack a dare and told him I would pay for it if he did it. Seated at the soda fountain counter with quick-witted Mrs. Klueckey herself asking for our order, Jack said, "We would like two crepe suzettes, if you have them, please."

She, spotting the humor in Jack's face, shot back, "Sold the last two yesterday, but I can give you two chocolate milkshakes if you'd like?"

"That would be fine," said Jack, "but you don't have to give them to us, my friend here is going to pay for them."

# A FIRST ASCENT WITH DENNY FOX

One of the best trips in my life was with Denny Fox. We were out to make the first ascent of an unclimbed mountain. In our college years we both followed the history and news of first ascents. There were more unclimbed peaks in those days and the average mountaineer still had a chance. You could dream about doing one, and we did. I am glad that it was with Denny that I had my chance. He was a perfect partner for me. A spiritual or philosophical mountaineer, he had read a great deal about climbing and was full of the history and ethos of the sport. However, it was Denny's special nature to believe that the only way he could deserve to enjoy this great beloved body of lore was to be a climber himself. He would not be a dilettante. He despised them. He would be real, authentic. So he climbed. I, in turn, enjoyed him a great deal and am sure that with no other person would this trip have been so much fun or have concluded with such unusual success.

Physically, Denny was thin, almost frail, and did not really look strong enough to hold up the weight of his always forward-jutting briar pipe. But he stood erect and looked you in the eye through the thick lenses of his permanent glasses. His wit was wry and acerbic, but he was a gentle and sweet person. He was undemonstrative—maybe even cool—but if you knew him you knew there were little sparkling fires of enthusiasm burning inside. He took after his mother, whom I much admired. She would sit in her Denver living room, knitting in a corner, and feigning deafness so that the group of young mountain climbers frequently assembled there would keep on talking without restraint. She had her own stories to tell about early Colorado, but she told me once that listening to us kept her alive.

Denny's father was another matter and not a comfortable one for Denny. His name was Rudolph. He was president of the Vulcan Iron Works, drove the largest Cadillac in Denver, and was a big and strong man himself. On a weekend trip to his mountain hideaway cabin, complete with a V8 diesel electric generator, he served huge steaks. Denny wasn't happy. He was a fastidious, almost delicate eater. He liked life to be spare, simple, lean. He told me once he wanted to die on the desert where his body would soon be desiccated and a few bleached bones and perhaps a single hard black turd would be his only memorial.

Denny and I had become friends in the Mountaineering Club at Yale. I admired his intellectual powers, and he, I think, appreciated my more practical competencies. Anyway, we had jointly hit on a great plan for our lives after graduation. We would go to Mexico and climb volcanoes. We viewed this as a career choice, obviating the need to suffer through job interviews with our classmates, and didn't even wait to attend graduation before setting off for Popocatepetl and those other white spires whose names I can no longer spell. I don't know how Rudolph took it, but now, fifty years later, I feel sorry that I deprived my father of attending a ceremony he would have enjoyed. As for the volcanoes, we did climb several (another story for another time), but Denny was turned back in midcourse that year by typhoid fever and I by the Marine Corps. It had been midsummer 1950 and an old Mexican man we met on the trail as we came down from a volcano excitedly told us our country was now fighting in a place I had never heard of. I had such difficulty understanding him that I asked him to scratch the name out with a stick in the black volcanic ash beneath our feet. KOREA.

Now, three years later, after the war, we got together again. I was still notably without a career plan. Denny had started the life of a scholar and was in graduate school; but he had, miraculously, researched a mountain that could possibly be a first ascent for us. This was very exciting. Who needs a career plan if you can go for a first ascent? I didn't. Such a mountain, however, could not be too tough as we were not the world's strongest climbers, and could not be too remote as Rudolph was not up for financing a major expedition unless it involved bulldozers and air compressors. Denny was against that. Could there still be such a mountain unclimbed in 1953? Denny had found it.

Attached to the North American continent there is a peninsula about eight hundred miles long and seventy-five miles wide. If the place is known at all it is known for its extremely inhospitable desert. But in this narrow peninsula there is a mountain range with elevations over ten thousand feet. Twice as high as the Adirondacks and not far below the Rockies or the Sierras. There is a high peak. This is Baja California and its Sierra San Pedro Martir. The upper slopes are forested, sometimes snowed upon, surrounded by desert and squeezed between the cool blue Pacific on the west and the shallow warm Sea of Cortez on the east. Cerro de la Encantada, the highest peak, was unclimbed.

Visiting the American Alpine Club headquarters in New York City, we found the first ascents of many lesser peaks all around the continent duly recorded in the club's ledgers. But there was nothing to indicate that La Encantada had ever been climbed. Across town at the New York Geographical Society there were some old maps but little worth having. Their staff helped us make up our own map on their special oilcloth from what little information they had. It showed mostly trails leading to abandoned mines and the supposed route of the Camino Real, the road between the early Spanish missions which the notes said recent explorers had been unable to find. La Encantada, the peak, was also called Picacho del Diablo on some maps and La Providencia on others. Its location varied from map to map by as much as ten miles. The only elevation given on any map was that of the peak, 10,126 feet. There were no contour lines.

At Denny's house in Denver we packed for the trip, spreading out on the lawn our climbing ropes, pitons and carabiners, boots and knapsacks, sleeping bags and cooking gear while the local kids watched and admired. It was summer, and at the peak's ten thousand feet we did not expect snow or ice, so we didn't pack winter gear; but other than that we had no idea of what this peak would demand in the way of equipment. We realized, but perhaps not adequately, that we would be making this ascent from sea level, climbing the full ten thousand feet. That's much more than is usual in the Rockies or Alps. We also realized that water would be critical so we packed extra army surplus canteens. The map indicated that some arroyos had water, "intermittently." Finally we shooed away all the neighborhood kids, stuffed everything into the car, and took off southwest for U.S. Route 66 and Baja California.

It was a funny feeling, after the three years in the Marine Corps, to be starting out again in the familiar old Ford with our much-used gear, a lot of it surplus from World War II, to climb another mountain. Was this going to work? It seemed we were going to step right back into the groove we had left on the way to our next volcano in 1950. Three years of grad school didn't seem to have changed Denny very much. He was always an intellectual. He knew a great deal about the things he was interested in, primarily medieval English literature, but he also knew mountain climbing, the desert, and race car driving. I was reminded of the last as we crossed the Continental Divide and he started us swooping down the great, steep, long curves of the Rockies' west slope. Because he knew, in this case because he had read, that race car drivers did it, Denny accelerated as we exited each curve. Fortunately the emergency brake in a Model A Ford is on the passenger side and I, less an intellectual, used it. We were always this way, different, but good friends. And if there was no change in his driving, I suspect that Denny, too, was also puzzling out whether we fit right back into our earlier college selves or had something changed. Was a first ascent still the same compelling goal now?

We began to go off course a bit in the first few days. The Kofa Mountains are a small range in southwestern Arizona with a storied history of desperate gold mining events and Denny wanted to make one quick detour to check out the spot. He had been told that an interesting place to start was Palm Canyon, where a short but steep rock climb led directly to a place of good interior access. We were not going to climb any peaks, just look around a bit. Bumping over a sandy desert road, we got there on the third evening by the light of the Ford's old and yellowing headlights. The mountain's rock wall sprang straight up out of the desert ahead of us. Four tall palm trees leaned against the rock. The temperature was 109 at exactly 9 p.m. The night before we had had a campfire on the windy Mogollon Rim, cooked a hot meal, gazed at the stars and gone to sleep. This night, after we had looked around and unpacked, it was still 109 degrees at 9:30. We couldn't face trying to cook so we ate bread and cheese and opened some beer. The beer was so hot that half of it squirted out of the can as soon as the opener penetrated it.

When I awoke the next morning, Denny was already sitting up against a palm tree reading *Beowulf*. *Beowulf* at seven o'clock in the morning in the desert with the temperature at 98 degrees, 11 degrees cooler than last night, but still warmer than anything Beowulf ever encountered. What we encountered shortly as we attempted the little exploratory climb up the rock wall was not what we had expected. The rock was smooth and uncomfortably warm. We were out of shape. We began to sweat. The route led up 30 or 40 feet into palm fronds rubbing against the rock face. How would we get by them? Were we supposed to hold on to them, push them aside, cut them off? This was going to be uncomfortable, maybe dangerous. We went back down, sweating even more. The Kofa Mountains, not really a goal for us anyway we had said, would remain unviolated. We left, drawn by thoughts of the pristine and forest clad Sierra San Pedro Martir with its summit peak, La Encantada, shimmering in cool heights above. Or maybe it was thoughts of a good breakfast in an air-conditioned restaurant in Yuma.

The one road down Baja California ran along the Pacific side, giving tantalizing glimpses of surf and the cool blue swells beyond. But the road seldom gets close enough that you can actually get out and swim, which you need to do often in Baja in the summer. The road after Ensenada was unpaved, bumpy, dusty, and hot. Furthermore, after about 75 miles down, we were supposed to be looking inland toward our mountains and the peak. All we could see so far were raw and uninviting foothills annoyingly high enough to obscure any view of the Sierra San Pedro Martir beyond. We started turning in at each little track we came to that seemed to head up a valley or inland toward the mountains. Many led nowhere. Possibly an abandoned adobe building and the remnants of fencing around a few acres that someone had once hoped were green but were now, anyway, a scorched tan soil supporting the growth of only a few yellowing cactus. At two or three road ends there were small inhabited ranches, the most conspicuous features of which were noisy chickens and children somehow surviving in the heat. We would discover that everything else, cattle and men, had slipped into darker, cooler shadows under roofs and trees, sometimes together. The arrival of a car was certainly an unusual event but would bring forth no person from the shadows. I spoke some Spanish but still felt challenged and uneasy about how to approach a man who, though awake, did not move forward or speak from his sequestered, cool, and shadowed resting place. What was he expecting? I moved slowly, kept my hands visible and gave submissive body language. At a distance of just a few yards we would be greeted with a quiet but pleasant sounding phrase or two. " Bueno," "Como sta," "Hace calor." But if it was pleasant, it was not informative. In response to our questions about how to get to the mountains, the most definitive answer was one we already knew. They were, and the men pointed, to the east of us. "Muy lejos." Very far. We had hoped they could show us on our map where we were; but taking the map in their hands they turned it around, looked at it, exclaimed, turned it over and looked at the back where the red, green, and blue ink had bled through in interesting patterns and they exclaimed again and held it up again in front of their faces, as if we had brought for them from the ocean a large and beautiful seashell.

This was 1953. We were not much more than 125 miles from San Diego. But it was an entirely different world. A cultural drop-off as steep as any mountain face. There were no paved roads, no gas stations, no stores of any sort, no U.S. license plates, and in fact no cars, only a few old trucks without plates from anywhere. There were no telephones, no power lines, and probably no radios. No one spoke English. And, beginning to worry us, where did you get water?

Believing we had reached the southern limit of where it any longer made sense to turn inward toward the mountains, we pulled off onto one of the dirt tracks heading inland and made camp in the late afternoon. Rattlesnakes immediately became the excitement. Big rattlesnakes and many of them. I had brought along an ancient single-shot .22 rifle, so for about an hour we shot them, as many of them as either of us had ever shot of anything. Perhaps ten. They we very warm and immobile from the sun and were easy to hit, but they were still a little scary to hunt among the clumps of sagebrush and cactus. Finally we got a monster, seventeen rattles, and decided to skin it. Denny wanted to try to cook and eat it, because that would be authentic. But we both quailed at the thought of actually trying to do it without any idea of how to proceed. No stories of climbing in the Alps or the Himalayas, or anywhere else for that matter, had any lore about how climbers had survived by eating rattlesnakes, much less instructions on cooking. So while Denny opened a can of beans for supper I carried the five foot long body of the snake, now skinned and very white and slippery, off a few feet into the sage and dropped it there.

I had sensed with our earlier defeat in palm tree climbing that our course to the summit of the Sierra San Pedro Martir was not going to be arrow like and might, in fact, be less than certain. What now happened, at about 3 in the morning, was also eventually to have its effect on the resolve needed for the final summit dash. After a couple of warm beers we had gone to sleep. Denny awoke with a full bladder, got up and stepped away from the camp to piss. Moving through the sage, his bare foot gently engaged the slimy, white, moonlit coils of the poisonous, reptilian corpse. Denny's heart stopped, his lungs exploded. I awoke, thinking we were being attacked. He would have shot me if he had had the strength left. But he didn't. By the time we could fall asleep again the sun was rising.

But the morning brought us good luck. Starting early on the way up our rattlesnake valley we soon found the ranch of Gregorio Vialobos, his wife, three young children and a large clutch of mixed animals. He had been more diffident when approached than others and had a serious demeanor. But he said he knew the mountains and even said it would be possible that he would guide us there. But standing around his stable while he did odd jobs, we struggled with our inability to get a firm commitment from him as to when we might leave and how long we might be gone. We were experiencing the "manana" problem. Finally, I sensed where the fulcrum was and asked, "Cuanto dolars necesita Usted para ir con nosotros a las montanas y a la picacho La Encantada?" After a pause, quietly but clearly, he said, "Cien dolars." I had the impression that though this was a brave and strong man it had taken all his courage to let his lips name such a large sum of money. I liked him. And how long would our trip take, I asked. It would take us a week, maybe two weeks. "Quien sabe?" But he would supply the food, horses, a mule, and some pack burros. We told him it sounded like a good deal to us. "Muy bien," I said, and with rising enthusiasm added, "Vamanos."

He had to make a trip in his truck to get some supplies and another saddle, but by mid afternoon he was back and had loaded the pack burros with several canvas and leather bags. He selected some items from our offered supplies—cooking oil, catsup, matches and a few cans of beef stew and one of condensed milk. He was anxious to get started, he said, because he wanted to get to a certain water hole before dark. He helped us load our gear and got us onto our mounts. Assembled in the yard before his house about to say goodbye, we heard his wife speak. She was standing in the door behind her oldest boy, about twelve or thirteen, with her hand on on his shoulder and said, "Quierre ir." He wants to go. Gregorio looked unhappy, thought hard for a moment and then with that smile of a father that comes with just that moment, said, "Bueno." The boy's face filled with light and his body with motion. In an instant he was beside us, bareback on his burro, his mother handing him a blanket and a parcel which she had had ready. Gregorio's serious demeanor returned as he gave the boy an appraising look. "Chaparreras," he said sternly. The boy dashed into the stable and back out again, strapping on around his waist and legs a pair of full-length, perfectly fitting, well-worn leather chaps. By the end of the trip we had had enough riding experience and had learned enough Spanish to say to each other, "Ojala que tenemos chaparreras!" Oh that we had chaps! It might have made a difference.

It took us two and a half hot, dry, brush-whipped days to reach paradise. Late in the afternoon of our third day we finally broke through the last brush and entered over a rim into an open forest of tall ponderosa pine. In it we were to discover many small sunny grasslands, some with trickles of cold water. Gregario called them *cienagas*. We were at the southwest corner of this high tableland, which rose gradually to the north for 30 miles and east for 10. Pointing that way, northeast, Gregorio said the peak lay there. And, yes, we would go that way. Manana.

The trip up had been difficult. While there were some trails, not very good ones, we were often bushwhacking over ridges and through gullies in an effort by Gregorio to link together a series of water holes that would actually have water at this midsummer date. We started traveling about four thirty in the morning and tried to be resting in shade near water during the midday hours. We dug for water in one critical spot. Slowly we learned why Gregorio knew his routes through this utter wasteland of cactus and brush as well as he did. He ran cattle, "gonados," in the upper grassland pastures and made a trip in the fall and spring to check on them and drive some down to sell or slaughter. But he didn't do this in midsummer. We could not possibly have made this trip, on foot or horseback, without his guidance and help. I am not sure anyone could have. Though neither of us were accustomed to riding much and our bottoms got painfully sore on our not-fancy saddles, it was our lack of chaps that caused the most problems. First our pants and then our legs were scratched, ripped and torn by cactus, thorns, and sharp brush. Later these cuts and scratches refused to heal, leaving our outer thighs and calves stiff and sore for days.

This campground we had reached the first night up on the forested plateau, about a mile or two into the big pines, was one that Gregorio used on his regular trips. There was actually a little shelter made of sticks tied and woven together with smaller split sticks and some bits of rope and twine. Its purpose was not human shelter but to keep food and supplies safe from smaller animals and rodents. But it looked picturesque and gave the camp a feel of permanence. It was under the branches of a particularly big ponderosa and in front of it was a big fireplace set up with rocks for cooking. The ground was flat and trodden down all around for some distance and one of the grassy meadows nearby had water.

Gregorio unpacked quickly and without saying a word was up on his horse and off again before we were really aware of it. Alejandro, the boy, now friendly and fun to have with us, said he did not know where his father had gone, but he had been told to light a fire and make corn bread. We did that and began to wonder what else we were going to eat for supper. All the beef stew and other ready food seemed to have been consumed on our trip up. The report of a rifle shot in a few minutes provided the answer. Within an hour of our arrival we were eating fresh venison roasted on iron pokers over the fire and hot pan-cooked corn bread washed down with the best water we had tasted in days.

Gregorio was also gone when we woke up the next morning. Alejandro still lay on the ground, wrapped in his one thin blanket with his feet toward the fire and his head resting on one of the leather saddlebags. When he woke I asked him, "A donde va su padre?" He responded with something like, "Es possible que el va a buscarme Tijuana." This sounded to me like, "It's possible he has gone to look for Tijuana." I had gotten very proud of my Spanish and was learning four or five new words a day. Alejandro was eagerly learning about ten or twenty English words a day, so we were closing in on the problem of accurate communication (Denny was best with *Beowulf*) but we were not there yet. If Gregorio had gone to Tijuana we were in trouble. But I had not detected that Tio Juan, his actual words, were the male gender and it was, in fact, Uncle John he had gone looking for. Gregorio, not one to waste information or words, had not told us about his wife's brother who lived up here year round and took care of the cattle. This was a surprise and hardly seemed credible until we met the man later in the day. Then it did seem credible.

The two of us were very glad to have as many hours of rest as possible. Walking was painful, as our outer legs were scabbed and ready to crack and bleed with any but the most gentle motion. So we took it easy. We had more venison and corn bread for breakfast, which was good but not quite as good as the coffee we had for breakfast every morning on this trip. This coffee actually got better and easier to make every day because of the unique nature of its transport. The leather saddlebag that was Alejandro's pillow held a large quantity of unground coffee beans and a goodly quantity of unground rock crystal sugar. Carried on the outer flank of Gregorio's horse, the bag and its contents were continually rubbed, pummeled and squeezed, in which process the sharp-edged sugar crystals ground up a certain amount of the coffee bean as well as a magically appropriate amount of themselves. One opened the saddlebag, took a spoon and carefully lifted out the needed amount of ground coffee and sugar, avoiding the unground beans which would be ready tomorrow, and put it in the coffeepot to boil. Denny, through silent communication, had somehow managed to acquire this job from Gregorio, who didn't give up much. Denny loved it and made great coffee. The next morning Tio Juan would show him one last additional component which made this drink the nectar, if not also the ambrosia, of this, our paradise in the Sierra San Pedro Martir.

The men arrived late in the afternoon driving in front of them a half dozen head of cattle, with calves at their sides, in true cowboy fashion and looking very much the part, swinging their braided rawhide riatas over their heads and yelling out commands in Spanish cow language. Tio Juan was tall and rangy. His movements had a sudden wildness about them that could be scary, but they were also graceful and effective movements. He moved cattle as another man might move lambs. Even at a distance, the look in his face said this was a different man. His eyes were directly on mine at twenty feet, his face was open, smiling, unguarded and expecting an intimacy that I hadn't yet got ready for. Though he was difficult to understand, he was talkative and emotional. Maybe he wasn't all there. But this place welcomed him, and he welcomed us, and he was soon a comfortable friend. Alejandro idolized him and Gregorio respected and valued him. He lived alone for many months, guarding and keeping track of the cattle. His hair and his clothes were that of a genuine mad man, except for his beautiful chaparreras. The parcel which Alejandro's mother had handed him as he mounted to leave on the trip included a small package of hard sugar candies for her brother's sweet tooth. A true sister. Gregorio had brought extra rice, beans, and corn for him. Also I noticed that that was where our catsup went. His main diet had to be game, but there may also have been trout.

Many things happened the next day, the day we thought was to be the last next day before heading for our first ascent. The first thing that happened was the coffee. It was now established that this was Denny's particular responsibility. Another duty was also becoming evident, that of providing Gregorio with small amounts of Balkan Sobraine pipe tobacco, Denny's lifelong love without which he might still be with us. It amused me to watch Gregorio carefully roll his cigarette with dirty brown scraps of paper and the world's most expensive pipe tobacco. When Denny had proudly announced that coffee was ready, waking us up early to enjoy the first cool rays of sunlight slipping in through the lower branches of the Ponderosa, Tio Juan jumped up fully dressed, the way he slept, and quickly herded a mother cow into the center of our little group around the fire. As Denny poured a cup of saddlebag coffee, Tio Juan grabbed it and held it under the udder of the cow and squeezed from a teat about three squirts of creamy, fresh milk into each cup and then passed one on to each of us. Alejandro got four squirts, in recognition that he was still growing. Breakfast enough.

Rounding up a few more head of cattle, Gregorio and Tio Juan then got into the real business of the day, branding all the young ones and castrating the males. Alejandro got practice in learning how to use his riata, I tried also to learn with Alejandro teaching me, and Denny, revealing the Vulcan Iron Works as his true lineage, kept the branding irons red hot. The men moved the cattle in, held them, branded and castrated them. The odor of singed hair and flesh was mixed with the pungent smoke from Denny's fire and swirled around our heads. The bleats and bellows of the young and unhappy new steers filled our ears. Denny's appreciation of the activity became intense. He had lost himself and the emotion of it showed. He told me that we were seeing a pure form of the way men and animals had related for eons. He had read a description in Beowulf. The culmination of the activity, around the fire as the evening began to darken, was close to ritual. Overseen by father and uncle, the testicles of a young steer were boiled in a pot and then one was presented to Alejandro to eat, which he did under the intense scrutiny of both father and uncle. They cheered and clapped when it was done, the father embracing the son briefly in a rare moment of revealed warmth. "Mucho hombre, Mucho Hombre, Mucho Hombre," we all found ourselves chanting, as if it had been scripted for us, with the firelight flickering on our proud and satisfied faces. Alejandro was transported. He walked around the fire gently sliding his outstretched arm across each of our backs as he went.

The next day turned out not to be the actual manana on which we had expected to head for the peak. That day was going to be manana. This day there was more cattle work to be done, so Denny and I struck out on foot to explore. We intended to get some needed exercise for our legs in preparation for the ascent, and to see if we could possibly find a location from which we could see the peak itself. Gregorio had been pessimistic about this but said if we went east to the plateau's rim we might be able to see the peak if we looked north. We had no altimeter but estimated that we were at about nine thousand feet so the peak would not be hugely higher than us. We thought we should be able to see it somewhere. We hiked east for three hours, gently climbing through wild evergreen forests and bits of open grassland and seeing no signs of humans, of cattle, or open vistas revealing the rim or the peak itself. Our map was useless.

When it was time to turn back we stopped to rest, sitting on a log in the shade at the edge of a sunny little *cienega* and felt more alone than on any other mountain trip we had ever been on. As we looked around, we asked the question that arises in places like this, "Has any other human being ever seen this spot?" We felt more certain than usual that the answer was no. Friends that we were, sitting silently there a little longer alone, we began to feel self-conscious in each other's presence. On the way back we shot a rabbit, and we ate him for supper since we had just about finished the venison.

Goodbye to Tio Juan, goodbye to the campground. The next morning Gregorio led us off heading north-northeast to the peak. After riding through similar country for about twenty miles and gently climbing about a thousand feet we stopped, sore and tired. No mountain. No peak. Gregorio said we would camp here and get to the peak tomorrow morning. We had boiled beans for supper, not even refried, no catsup. The corn, rice and venison were gone. Despite several sorties in search of another deer, Gregorio had been unable to spot one. He was disturbed by this but you had to know him to see it in his impassive face. He took out of his personal pack a very small bottle of very hot sauce and put some on his beans, then offered it to us. The beans were better.

We had beans and coffee for breakfast. From the same pack Gregorio now brought out the can of condensed milk. Had he been saving it for this, our most important day? At about eleven-thirty we finally got to the plateau's eastern rim. It was exciting to feel it coming, on our right, with the air lightening, the sky brightening, the silent sound of the huge drop off of thousands of feet of space raising the hairs on the back of our necks. We dismounted to walk the last hundred feet to the edge. There it was beneath us, the Desierto de San Fermin and the Sea of Cortez beyond, steaming and hazy. Gregorio, standing beside us, became excited and began pointing and calling our attention to the north. "Mira, mira, alli, alli, el picacho, la cumbre!" (Look, look, there, there, the peak, the summit.) A quarter of a mile, to give Gregorio due credit for his navigational skills, up along the rim and standing about eight hundred feet east of and separate from the rim was a little butte, almost a horn, about one hundred feet higher at its top than the rim itself of which it had obviously once been part before erosion had separated it from the main body of rim rock. This was the peak? This was the peak. What a surprise, what a disappointment. It was just that it wasn't like anything we had imagined or visualized. I think we had both been thinking about something a little more like the Matterhorn, but maybe not quite so big and steep. The whole process of adjusting dreams to reality was intensely going on in our heads. We walked along the rim to a point opposite the peak and lay down on our elbows at the edge looking out at it.

"What the hell."

"Christ."

"I can't believe it"

"Well, it begins to make sense," Denny said. "This is why nobody knows anything about it, and why we couldn't see it from anywhere until we got here."

"Why the hell didn't Gregorio tell us what it was like?"

"God, I don't know," Denny responded. "Maybe he thought we wouldn't pay him to take us here if we knew what it was like."

"No, I don't think so. He didn't have any way of knowing what we were expecting, what we were hoping for. For him this is probably one hell of a big deal peak. Look how excited he was when he saw it."

"Yeah, I guess you're right. He's a good guy."

"Are we going to climb it?" I pose the big question.

"Who wants to know?"

"You mean, who would ever know?"

"You mean, if we did or not?"

"Yeah."

Denny, studying what would be our route, says, "Look at that cactus and that thorn brush. I never saw it so thick, even the stuff we came through on the way up on the other side."

"Yeah. What's the drop, about four hundred feet down to the saddle?"

"About that. Maybe more. The rock under the brush where you can see it doesn't look too bad. We would need the rope for that last pitch. Close to vertical. How long do you think it would take?"

"I don't want to think. I don't want to do it," I tell him.

"I don't either."

After a moment I say, "But we should."

"Yeah, I know."

"After all, it is the highest peak in the country."

"Baja California is not a country," the scholar corrects me.

"I forgot."

"Will we kick ourselves forever if we don't do it?"

I duck the question and assert, "If we poke a cactus in our eye we'll kick ourselves forever. Can you see it written up in the Club Journal of Mountaineering Accidents in 1953?"

"Yeah, but it would still be a first ascent."

"Christ, I don't know. Would they ever even write this thing up?"

"You know," he says, and I can tell some philosophy is coming, "there's another way of looking at this. If we did it, then all

the rest of our lives we'd be the guys— we'd always think of ourselves as the guys, who made a first ascent somewhere and we
wouldn't know what to do with ourselves afterwards, we
wouldn't do anything, because we had already done the big
thing."

"You're too sophisticated. Next you are going to tell me about
being and becoming."

"Exactly."

"Well," I tell him, "I think I know what you mean. But what
I'm trying to imagine is writing this up or trying to tell it as the
story of a real first ascent. They'd laugh. Let's face it--climbing
this isn't going to impress anybody, not even ourselves."

"Then why are we doing it? And if you tell me 'because it's
there' I'll york."

"Because if we don't we'll know what kind of guys we are,
and——"

Gregorio arrives and stands silently a few feet behind us. I tell
him we are trying to make up our minds whether to climb the
peak. He offers nothing. I ask him if he could probably get water
and a deer for supper while we climb the peak and then could he
have things ready for us when we got back. He answers none of
this, but after a few moments says, without emotion, "Hay peligro." There is danger. I don't know how to read the man. Mexicans don't say just "Hay peligro", they always say "Hay mucho
peligro." Even more difficult, I don't know how to read myself. I
don't know what I want to do, and I don't think Denny does either.

Alejandro has tied up the pack animals and now arrives. To
our amusement he abandons his usual modesty about such
things and stands there, as every other boy in the world would,
pissing off the edge of the first big cliff he has ever seen.

I ask Gregorio what kind of danger is he talking about.

He responds with, "Hace mucho calor, no hay agua, hay
mucho espino y matoral, y tambien serpientes de cascabel."

Denny doesn't need a translation because its pretty easy to get the idea, especially with Gregorio's serious tone of voice, but Denny does catch one thing I might not have translated and yells out, "Serpents! What kind of serpents are *cascabels*?"

Alejandro, excited, screams back with a word I had recently taught him, "Rattlesnakes!"

Silence.

"How about let's not and say we did," says one.

"How about pissing on it," says the other.

Relieved and relaxed, smiling in appreciation of each other's congenial thinking, we get up together, stand at the rim and proceed to piss over the edge. Alejandro laughs delightedly and Gregorio gives us the only full smile he's shown on the whole trip. The peak remains unclimbed.

+++++++++++++

As you can perhaps imagine, versions of this story with different endings have been told by at least one of us, I know for sure, but I suspect by two of us. Under the duress of social competition and the influence of alcohol, mountain climbers are the brothers of fishermen. But the version now in your hand is the true one. It was written forty seven years after the trip by the surviving member of the summit team, Walter N. Morrison, for the fun of it and to honor the memory of his climbing companion and sorely missed friend Denton Fox.

Modern guide books, of which there were, thankfully, none available that we could find in 1953, record the peak to have been first scaled in 1923 by a Mexican government survey team. There appears to have been at least two other successful parties before us, and a book written about an attempt after us tells the story of a spectacular failure. Although not many people do, you can now drive to within a few miles of the peak over a poor gravel road that ends at an observatory and telescope maintained by the Mexican government. The land, our paradise, is now a National Park.

# REUNION

"Use the hot water, it'll cool you off better," John ordered me as we stood side by side, naked, two nearly identical- looking 24 year-old Marine Corps Privates in the big shower room at Quantico, Virginia, midsummer 1951.

"You're crazy. Cool water can carry away more heat," I responded, and was thinking John was like that. He believed things, things he'd been told. Probably believed you could make ice cubes quicker with hot water than cold. I'd heard that, too.

"Now you listen to me, Wally. Up there where you come from in Yankee land you don't know anything at all about hot. When you're real hot, like we are now, and you want to get cooled off for the evening activities, you take a hot shower. It'll last you longer into the night. You'll see."

I was the only New Englander in our group and John loved to call me "the Yankee." He was "the Rebel," from Tennessee. Everybody called him that, "the Reb," and they often spoke of us together as "the Yank and the Reb twins." We had become buddies. I liked John a lot.

"OK, John, I'll try it," I said, and I turned down the cold water and turned up the hot. The proof of the idea did not become noticeably evident to me that night on liberty, nor has it ever finally established itself, but I have not taken a shower on a hot summer day for the fifty years since without turning the hot water up a bit, even if just a little in recent years, and remembering John Pennington.

At this time the Korean War was about a year old and the Marine Corps' First Division had taken a terrible beating the first winter at the Chosin Reservoir under the careless direction of General Douglas MacArthur. Marine Corps morale improved greatly when President Truman relieved MacArthur of command, but the Division still needed replacements in all ranks, especially 2nd Lieutenant infantry platoon leaders. That's where John and I came in, along with the 150 or so others in our group, all of whom had been in the enlisted ranks. We made up the 5th Special Basic Officers Candidate School. The war now looked like it was going to last a while and it was hoped that those of us who could graduate from this rigorous training and testing would be in Korea in time to lead platoons in the second winter.

We had come into this program in different ways. In my case, I had been in the Marine Corps in 1945, the last year of World War II, and had gone to basic training at Parris Island, but after the war ended I was discharged without having served a full year of duty. I went into the Merchant Marine for six months and then to college for four years. As the Korean War started in 1950, men with my brief service history would be drafted to serve again. I wasn't at all happy about this, which is putting it mildly, but I had done well in boot camp at Parris Island and liked and respected the Marine Corps so I joined their ranks again as a Private and felt that at least I was returning to a friendly place. I was lucky in my first assignment and served at Quantico during the winter of 1950-51 as clerk to the Commandant of The Marine Corps Schools, Colonel Wallace Martin Greene, a very good man who later became Commandant of the Marine Corps and then the Marine Corps member of of the Joint Chiefs of Staff. As a fresh Yale College graduate, I did a good job for him as his clerk. He liked me, and he arranged for me to take the General Military Science Aptitude Test on which, he said, I got about the highest score he had ever seen. I was made proud, but equally scared. He sent me off to Officer Candidate School.

John and I became friends during the very first weeks when we discovered that on every forced march or long cross country hike we came in together and usually ahead of everybody else. We were built identically with long striding legs, tough feet, and plenty of wind. If nature had given us this similarity, our family backgrounds had given us something else important in the Marine Corps: familiarity and comfort with rifles and pistols and the ability to shoot them well enough to usually get Expert scores. In my case, shooting and hand loading had been my father's hobby, he had been captain of the rifle team at Yale, and he had taught me to shoot well. I had learned on the Springfield 30-'06 First World War standard issue rifle that he had carried in France and a Colt 45 caliber Military Service revolver. I can no longer remember for sure much of John's earlier background, but most importantly, that background included a lot of squirrel hunting in the Great Smoky Mountains. What I do still remember is that when he threw a rifle to his shoulder for shooting in the offhand standing position it was quicker and more accurate than anyone, and had the grace of a athlete throwing perhaps a baseball or a javelin. His shooting position was not fully Marine Corps standard in that the axis of his left arm was not quite vertical nor his right elbow quite horizontal and he was hunched just slightly forward rather than fully erect, but it was obviously so well practiced and naturally beautiful that no instructor ever called him on it. I picture him as having descended from a gentlemanly line of Kentucky backwoods riflemen, perhaps even Daniel Boone. We could both take apart and put back together the many pieces of our M1 Garand rifles blindfolded in record times and enjoyed doing it.

On our first liberty together in D.C. we found the downstairs bar at the Sheraton Hotel. It became our headquarters for the summer where we met other Marines, the girls we picked up that eventually became regular friends, and even a senator who wanted to talk to us. After a hot, dirty, and tiring week of training at Quantico, this bar, dark and cool with comfortable seats gathered about round tables and with waiters always ready to bring sharp looking young Marines in crisply pressed khakis another round of frosty Tom Collins and a bowl of snacks, was a paradise we thought about all week long. And it was here that we became truly good friends.

We discussed the war. Did we think the U.S. was doing the right thing? While we had questions, they were certainly not of the intensity of the next generation's about Vietnam. The domino theory—does anyone still remember, that the West could not allow one country to be pushed into communism for fear that all the next in line would fall down, too—was the central rationalization for the war. Well, we had played with dominoes, as had most people, and, well, dominoes do tip each other over, don't they? Ultimately we both bought into the idea that we would fight for the Marine Corps and to uphold its unique reputation and not try to answer the imponderable questions facing the nation. We were glad we were not in the Army. But most importantly, on our second night at the Sheraton, we got close enough to admit to each other that we were scared about getting killed or wounded in Korea and scared about taking command of an infantry platoon of 30 or so combat veterans perhaps under fire the very moment of one's arrival. I so admired John, his high spirits, his good looks, his skills and wit, that I had not believed he had these unmentionable, if not forbidden feelings, and I felt warmly grateful to him for letting me know that I was not alone. With no further words we became each other's secret sharer and best friend.

But the Marine Corps has been around awhile, and it knows all about these fears and has a way to help you with them and at the same time accomplish its goals. The challenge to graduate from Officer Candidate School is so great and the reward is made to seem, and is, so golden (lieutenant's bars), and the results of failure so ignominious, that one's entire mental and physical activity is soon focused on the difficult but nonetheless achievable goal of becoming a good officer. There simply is no time or energy left to worry about getting killed. Or at least not very much. War-making depends, successfully, on the efficacy of this formula. It has always worked, and I think always will.

Our days started with a 6 a.m. reveille—except when they woke us at 3 a.m. to lead a night patrol through the woods following a compass azimuth (this test did sort people out) with a gruesome course of physical exercises followed by four or so hours of classroom work in the morning. The instructors were officers who had fought at Guadalcanal, Iwo Jimo, The Reservoir. We sat in uncomfortable folding chairs in hot Quanset huts or pine board buildings with no fans or air conditioning, but we listened to these men because we knew our lives depended on it. The subjects ranged from field sanitation practice to leadership. In between were the use of mortars, how to set up ambushes, machine gun fields of fire, assault tactics, the gathering and use of intelligence, maps and how to read and use them, communication and coordination with other units, and probably lots more I have now forgotten. In the afternoons we would go into the field and actually do and practice the morning's lessons. In some situations one of us would be designated a leader, perhaps to set up an ambush using the other candidates as his troops. Another candidate would have been designated to lead a scouting enemy patrol. Would the patrol leader be sharp enough to avoid ambush or would it have been set so skillfully that he was trapped? The training officers evaluated our performance. These were miniature war games and John and I were both good at them. With others we would critique and discuss them late into the evenings, much as some men love to do the same with football games. I still, today, see terrain in military terms, am instinctively anxious about being in places that lend themselves to ambush, and am not above noting, to myself, what a wonderful grazing field of fire could be set up on a peaceful New Hampshire hillside pasture while walking across it on a Sunday afternoon. A great deal of my mental furniture, processing techniques, and memories were established during this training course, perhaps as much as that which became embedded in me later in actual situations in Korea: Know the objective, keep the schedule, coordinate, prioritize. The men eat first in the chow line, you pay each one personally, by name, on payday, look sharp, every rifle always clean, always, and other good old marine traditions. Always.

A Fifth of Gin, Gilbey's London Dry Gin, in a square, frosted glass bottle with its distinctive label, is also embedded in my memory from this summer. We had purchased an old second-hand car together, a 1937 Dodge, and I sat anxiously in it, double parked, while John ran into the package store to buy the liquor. It was his choice. I chose the Dodge, he chose the Gilbey's. It was to become our standard weekend fare, along with a couple of quarts of grape juice, paper cups, and a bag of ice cubes. Later, when we found the girls, we sometimes bought two bottles, but always Gilbey's London Dry. Mixed with the grape juice, the girls called it purple Jesus. Memory is so demanding of its right to be inviolate that even now I can't, or anyway I haven't since that summer, bought Gilbey's Gin for fear of disturbing these old memories with new associations.

John gets the credit for finding the girls. After a few false starts with women who were not much more than streetwalkers, he convinced a party of four girls having a drink at the Sheraton that they should not wait any longer for their expected party of four sailors. His line, of course, was that two Marines were as good as four sailors. Shortly all six of us were in the old Dodge careening around Washington, singing songs, spilling grape juice, and making friends. I remember I drove around DuPont Circle three times in a row just for the exhilaration of it. If I die now I won't feel cheated of great moments. The girls were college grads about our age starting office jobs with large government agencies, shared an apartment together, and if I remember anything distinctive about them it was that they were good sports. We spent weekends together, usually the four of them with us but sometimes just two or three. We went once to Harpers Ferry to see the historic site, and once we went as far south as Virginia Beach where we swam, had a bonfire, and slept all night on the sea-lapped sand. One of our favorite places to go was the Falls of the Potomac which was then, at least, a long patch of low grass running up and down along the Potomac River as it tumbled over rocky outcrops and drop-offs. We drank Purple Jesuses, floated paper cups down the river, played ball, chased each other and fell down in the grass and kissed. We did more than kiss, but not much more. Nobody fell in love. Somehow the pairing off of uneven numbers worked and we had a good time. John and I were about matched in how much we wanted, dared ask for, and needed from girls at that time. We were really both pretty young. John had a certain boyish form of the Southern gentleman's solicitous and gentle approach to women that I admired and tried to emulate.

I think often of these things, and other events of that summer leading up to our graduation. Perhaps I have thought about John in some way as often as once every day for 50 years. Who knows? How often do you think of anybody from your past? Your first madly loved girlfriend? Your mother? It's hard to figure.

But now a surprise phone call from another member of our training group has suddenly changed the routines of my memory. There is going to be a fiftieth anniversary of our class at Quantico this summer, 2001. Someone will send me a sign-up list and the list of everybody they have located and the ones they are still looking for. I had never dreamed of such a thing. My Marine Corps experience is a totally finished thing, locked up and put away. And though I very often visit memories of it, particularly of the 1951 summer, I have never met or communicated with another Marine with whom I served. I feel a disturbance in my mind at the prospect of such meetings. Even my body is talking to me. It wants to know if it is also going back there with me? Well, I say to it, I promise you that if we go you won't have to carry a pack or a rifle. But do I want to go? And, really, do I want to see John again?

At the end of summer we did both successfully graduate from the Officer Candidate School and were commissioned as 2nd lieutenants. After a two weeks' leave at home we both went to Korea as infantry platoon leaders, but were assigned to different units and we never saw each other again after Quantico.

A year or so after the war when I was still in the Reserves in Washington state, I checked the records once to see where John was. The report said that he had been badly wounded in Korea but was now home in the U.S. Those were not the days of transcontinental telephone calls. I guess I didn't have an address. I didn't make contact with him. I was busy starting a logging and sawmill empire, or so I hoped. And then life sucked me on until here I am now, in still water, nudged by a possible reunion meeting, and thinking of all these things.

I do, sometimes, but not often, have a touch of survivor guilt when I think of John wounded and my having escaped unhurt. It hits me only briefly. He survived. But it is painful because the way I see John wounded is not in his bloody battle clothes as I saw others, but naked, the wounds and blood on his naked body. We were close, we shared back then, we share now.

But, happily, it is more often that I think of our training adventures together such as our joint solution to what was known as "the heavy jeep problem". Four of us, officer candidates, were taken to a steep, narrow, dry gully out behind some maintenance buildings where there was a large jumbled collection of abandoned construction material and broken equipment. Parked a few feet back from the edge of the gully was a beat-up jeep with about fifteen 5-gallon jerry cans full of diesel fuel loaded into and on it. There were three training officers, unusual in itself, a major and a captain sitting in deck chairs in the shade across the gully with clipboards, pads of paper, and pencils in hand for scoring purposes and another captain now giving us our instructions:

"Three of our light tanks are 4 miles up the road, across this gully. They are retreating. The Chinks have some antitank rockets. The tanks have run out of fuel. There is enough diesel loaded on this jeep to get them back safe. Get it to them quick. The front-wheel drive on the jeep is broken. All you have is rear-wheel drive. Start."

My heart was pounding before the captain had finished. Since they hadn't designated one, they were looking for leaders and cooperativeness. But also, of course, who could figure out the best way to get the jeep across. I should be able to do the latter, it was a kind of thing I was usually good at.

Standing at the edge of the gully I yelled out, "Hey, no matter whether we try to drive the jeep down the gully and up the other side, or we try to build a bridge out of some of this junk, we should first hand-carry the jerry cans across to lighten the load."

"Right," yelled John. "Charlie, grab some with me and let's go!"

I had already decided that the jeep wouldn't make it up the other side, even though I thought I saw some disguised wheel tracks in the gully. "Martin," I said, "Let's go find some stuff to build a bridge." Martin was a small, intellectual, very nice guy.

After surveying what we had, it came down to how best to make use of a collection of old wooden forklift pallets. We could easily pile them up in the center of the gully, if there were enough, to build a support with them for the not very strong stringers we had found, or we could use them as decking on the stringers. But there was barely enough for either job alone, not both. An alternative for decking was a small collection of warped old boards, not enough of them really, and maybe not strong enough. I pictured the jeep progressing one board at a time while we took them from behind the wheels and moved them to the front. The gully was at least ten feet deep. What would we stand on while doing this fun job. Who would be driving? I didn't like the thought. I grabbed the top end of a small old telephone pole we had found, Martin right after me, and we dragged it to the gully. John and Charlie, poking their heads up over the gully edge, saw it coming, complete with cross-arm still on it and dangling wires.

"Man, is this the best kind of beam you guys can find?" exclaimed Charlie. "Maybe we should try to drive the jeep down and push it up the other side." Charlie was the strongest of the four of us.

"It was the only one the Phone Company would sell us," said Martin. "Wait till you see the other one."

John had grabbed the cross-arm and had already reached the bottom of the gully pulling the pole down behind him. "Come on, Charlie; you're the only one that's strong enough to lift this end up to the top."

Martin and I brought the other beam, a good looking 4x6, but really of questionable strength to hold up one side of a jeep on a span of 20 or more feet. We planned it to be on the right-hand side so the telephone pole would carry the heavier driver's side on the left.

"Christ, it's too short," we all cried at once as we carried the 4x6 out to place it across the gully. "We can build a little abutment for it right here on this bank and then it will reach." Using an old 50 gallon oil drum for the upright we had it done in a minute and bridged the remaining gap with a short beam. Martin and John were already carrying the wooden pallets and putting them in place for our bridge deck. Charley and I were putting in position under the 4x6 the one strong upright support post we could find. It was going to have to be held and steadied as the jeep passed over. John was already in the jeep and had turned the motor on. He looked down over the edge at me and yelled,

"Morrison, will this here thing you call a bridge really hold me?"

"Yes, keep to the left over the pole and you'll make it, John," I answered.

John believed me. He had started moving the jeep gently forward and got the front wheels up onto the first pallet when the major, across the gully, stood up and cried out, "OK, you men, you've got it right. Good job. That's it. You can quit now."

After a moment or two of complete silence we all heard John slowly say a disrespectful two-syllable word. But he said it with four soft, Rebel syllables and in such a tone that I thought maybe he might escape court-martial. "Buull-shiit," a pause, and then, louder, "Major, I request permission to advance toward the enemy."

There was another equally long silence and then, "Permission granted."

John then drove to the middle and stopped. We all cheered and clapped, including the major who had probably never before been addressed to his face with the word bullshit. Only John.

The letter about the reunion and the lists comes. The first page shows that only about twenty-five guys have signed up so far to go. John has not signed up. I realize I still didn't know if I want to go. The second page has the names of the guys they have located and been invited, including mine, and shows their addresses, and the next page the names of the many still unlocated. John's name is not on the second page. And not on the third page. There is another, last page. About thirty names, with one word after each. Deceased. About three quarters of the way down, where the Ps always are, my eyes go straight to it and see no other. John Pennington, Deceased.

I'm thinking, John, where the hell are you all of a sudden? I'm having trouble finding you. You can't be gone. I would have known. Did you go all the way across the bridge? You knew he couldn't say no. Are you taking the diesel up that road? Wait up. Wait up. I'm coming across too. Wait up. I'll go and get a bottle of Gilbey's. Wait for me.

## MAYBE NEXT YEAR

"Jimmer, want to go out tonight?" Jimmer he calls me. "No wind, the tide will be right. Got the bilge pump fixed."

"You mean the tide will be coming in?" I ask. Don't want to be out there at dusk with the tide going out. Motor quits too much. Louie, that's him, says this fall we'll trade the boat in and get a new one. He's said that before. I'll be surprised. Boat's been around longer than any woman. But the other day he actually took me to look at a new Aquasport. It could happen.

"Yeah, we'll get the last hour or two of the incoming tide. We could fish Jeremy Point. I hear they're catching big stripers, big ones, out in the bay. A couple might come in to us at the point and we'd get a keeper. I've had enough small bass and enough blues for this year."

"Yeah, that sounds good. Great, Louie. Probably be our last time out this fall. Season's ending. Getting dark out there. Meet you at five at the dock?"

"Yeah, that's about right. See you there." He knows I like Jeremy. It's my favorite place. I tell my wife, she always wants to know, we're just going fishing again. She worries.

I guess she's right, sometimes anyway. When you're in Louie's old wooden boat Wellfleet's big bay can have enough adventure to keep us old guys feeling like kids again, but we do get in trouble, too. Last time out we were looking for the submerged continent of Atlantis, only here its called Billingsgate. We hit it. Big rocks, the old foundations of a town that was here 150 years ago.

There were 30 families, with houses and children, a church with a graveyard, all washed away now. Maybe we hit a gravestone. We sprung open the leak again where the propeller shaft goes out, but we took turns bailing to help the bilge pump and we didn't sink. We know how to keep the old inboard motor going most of the time and to keep afloat, but with a new outboard you could turn sharper corners and raise the propeller up, which is probably what we need if we're going to keep doing this much longer.

Jeremy Point where we like to fish is near Billingsgate. It's at the end of a protecting sandbar where you can feel the whole Atlantic ocean pushing in and where, after a time of peaceful rest, you know the tide has suddenly turned and out goes all the harbor water, seaweed, floating logs, dead fish and all. In the evening families of seals crawl up to rest here, the old bulls hanging out together. Further out in Cape Cod Bay the sunset comes on under a long, low tent of dark rose-colored cloud reaching north to the open Atlantic. The last rays leave a small haven of glistening brightness on the water in the further distance. When the birds finally settle down on the sandbar, evenly spaced in a long row to sleep, after a while one gull will leave his spot without a sound and fly northwest into the sunset, across the empty bay, no shore in sight. Without a voice, the gull's flight alone asks you to follow, just as the liquid notes of the unseen wood thrush on a summer evening at the edge of a forest call you in to darkness. A place of escape and peace. We both like it.

The old motor coughs and gurgles but pulls us steadily toward this favored place once again. Louie, never a hat or dark glasses, gives me the wheel, as he usually does, and starts coiling up a stiff old piece of hemp anchor line. "But you know", he says, and obviously has been thinking, "any newer boat I trade this in for will have one of those electronic radar fish finders on it. That Aquasport had one. Are you thinking you and I would use one of them? Have you thought about that?"

"No, can't say I have. Knowing us, we probably couldn't understand how to make it work."

"Yeah, well, I've been thinking about it. Couldn't figure out what I didn't like, but it finally came to me. If you had a fish on, and he gave you a real nice, sporting fight, but in the end you got him in and landed him, would you be able to look that fish in the eye and feel proud of what you had just done, knowing that you had located him, found him out, using that electronic thing? I wouldn't."

I had only a moment to picture Louie looking that fish in the eye—one eye at a time I guess—and was starting to tell him that I agreed with him, that it was unnatural, upset things, the balance of nature, when suddenly Louie, now squinting ahead into the low sun cries out, "Look! Birds working, lots of birds working, right at Jeremy Point. Hot stuff. Give her the gas, Jimmer. We've got fishing tonight!"

I push the throttle up, giving her as much gas as she will take, but we aren't speedy. We head for the point and just hope the birds are still diving when we make it. It could be a real feeding frenzy.

They can happen anywhere, but most often at tide races like Jeremy. The sign we watch for is birds working. And Louie always sees them first. It starts when plankton and other small food suspended in the fast tidal currents moving past the point slow down and drop out into the stiller water behind the point. That makes a feast for the small bait fish often schooling there. Larger, predatory fish soon race in with snapping jaws and gorge themselves on the bait fish. Many snapped-off pieces float to the surface uneaten. Terns and seagulls, from great distance, see these shiny morsels, the debris of undevoured fish, and assemble overhead to drop and dive into the melee below. Sometimes a small fish, in eagerness to escape the jaws of a bass or bluefish, will dart to the surface, or even jump out of the water, and make itself an easy target for the bird. The bird, then rising heavily with a frightened five-inch mackerel in its beak, will be attacked by its brethren trying to grab the meal. The mackerel will fall out of the beak, back to the sea. The bluefish will bite half of it off and gulp it down. The bird will dive again, almost too close to the blue, and grab the mackerel's other half and swallow it in ascending flight. More blues arrive. The gulls and terns are frantic with hunger, fun, and screaming. Five dive at one time. The water begins to boil and soon is covered with an oily film from chewed-up mackerel. Now, finally, all but the biggest members of this fighting food chain are here. But we are coming, too. We're coming. Two aged hominids, boat borne, fishermen. Wait for us. We're coming!

We're coming to cast our mackerel-like lures into the oily, roiling circle under the birds hovering wings and screaming cries, and to do our appointed part and take a fish; we, the highest members of the chain, playing the ultimate role. Or at least, so we hominids think.

We arrive in time, and find the feeding frenzy is taking place on the outer side of the point, over the bar. The tide is going out now, no longer coming safely in. Louie's timing has been off by a couple of hours, but we head straight out over the bar for the action anyway. Louie yells to cut the motor and let the strong current carry us silently out to the fish. I do this and grab a rod to be ready for the first cast. I look down and see the gravel of the bar pass swiftly beneath us. We stand poised and ready to cast as soon as the current brings us to these fish. Excited anticipation is often so great that a first cast is wild, or so strong it snaps the lure off, or backlashes in a mess of tangled line. But we are cool, and at 150 feet we both whip our plugs into the very center of the melee. Within seconds we see large fish lunge toward both plugs, taking them down with great power beneath the surface. We're on! A fight! And it is not unevenly matched. These fish are big, and in a hurry. The release drags on the reels are overpowered and the spinning click of fast, out-racing line is the music we love to hear.

But we are stronger, the tackle holds, and soon we have two very large blues at the stern. Gaffed and in a barrel there is immediately enough fat bluefish to make fillets for several families. Anxious to get a bass if they're here also, we don't take the time to remove the barbed treble hooks from the sharp-toothed mouths of blues, but cut the lines and tie on new plugs. This time we use only barbless single or double hooks. It's quicker to catch and release fish and with no harm to them. The birds are diving all around us with an increased frenzy and sometimes dive mistakenly at our plugs. We see the bigger fish racing by us in pursuit of the frantic, darting bait fish. The scene is such a powerful, savage, unleashed phenomenon of nature, oblivious of us, that it almost seems we have mistakenly verged into the middle of a small thunderstorm. But we belong here, too. Elsewhere in the world birds steal from the butterfly-shaped fishnets extended by hungry Mexicans, eagles and bears contest with Indians at the best salmon-spearing rapids, and gulls scream and squall around the laden trawlers returning to the ports of all the world. We belong here.

Then we begin to hook some bass. We catch a fish on almost every cast. It seems each one one is bigger than the last. Neither of us has caught a 32-inch bass in a long time, so we hold each one up over the transom to measure it; but although we have many at 28, 29 and 30 inches, no larger one takes a lure. We begin to tire and it's getting dark. Suddenly we are casting and nothing takes the lure. It's over. The birds are silent. The fish are down, or gone. One last cast each, into dead and lifeless water, and we know we are through.

We sit and rest a moment, uttering modest exclamations, both feeling the same pleasure and satiation. "Well," I finally say, "We didn't get the big bass. I thought we were going to, but we didn't."

"No we didn't. We didn't get him. Not this year. But maybe next year," says Louie.

We are sitting quietly in the back eddy behind the point, the old boat peaceful on the glassy water in the late sunset. In earlier years, younger years, we would have had a smoke. Over on the bar I see the gulls settling down for the night in their regimented row. I'm wondering if one of them pretty soon will flap off, out over the bay, alone. I watch. It's late for travel. I ask Louie. "Where do they go?"

"Who knows. They don't feed this late. It's eerie, strange. You notice when one of them goes it leaves an empty space. The others don't fill it in. But, hell, Jimmer, we've got to get out of here or we'll be the ones spending the night out there. Crank it up and let's get going."

We both laugh, and then I tell him, "Some night, in the end, Louie, I just want to drift out there, into the sunset, like those birds, following them. I know for damn sure that in this boat after a while we would go down, sink down, for good and ever. Out in that bright spot, see it? How can it be so bright when the sun has set, and all around it it is so dark? It would be dark by the time we got there, I suppose."

"Yeah, it would be dark in the end," he says thoughtfully, "but I'd go. Follow those birds. See where they go. Quiet out there. No lights. Maybe we shouldn't wait too long."

But now we're heading back and moving along pretty well. At the bar we see the tide is racing out under us and we are really making only slow forward progress. The tide is a lot lower than we thought. I aim the boat carefully for what I think is the deepest crossing place and hope the propeller doesn't hit bottom. But it does. We begin to churn gravel. If we had an outboard we would just raise it up a bit. But we can't.

"Louie, the prop's hitting bottom."

"Yeah, I know. I can hear it. But, Christ, we've got to get through. It's practically dark. Listen, it's just small gravel. Give it the gas hard and we'll push through."

I do and we keep moving, but the sound and feel is pretty rough. Like a cement mixer. What are we doing to the prop? Louie rushes up to the bow to take weight off the stern. We move along better, but the sound is still gruesome.

"Shall I keep going?"

"Yeah, Christ, we got to. We can't quit now. Keep going."

Considering the damage we must be doing, Louie doesn't look or sound too unhappy. It seems to me we're killing the boat. But the sound eases and we're over the bar. So I head us back for the inner harbor and the dock, but I can tell from the vibrations shuddering up through the hull and from our slow speed that the old brass prop is mostly chewed off.

"Well," says Louie, and I detect a note of glee in his voice, "I guess we won't be trading her in this year. Nobody will want it running like this. We'll have to get that prop fixed over the winter. Couldn't make a deal on her the way she is. Not this year."

"Yeah, that's right. But maybe next year."

# CLYDE'S WAKE

Clyde Davis, big, strong, talkative, 84 year old retired logger, died Saturday morning. He was getting out of his car beside the house, and, as everybody at the wake said, had just finished doing his favorite thing, driving around town in his car. He collapsed on the garden earth by the driveway, which would have been mud two weeks before but now, with spring, smelled good and would soon show daffodils. His wife Ada told us how she tried to help him, to prop him up a little so he could breath better. But he weighed 250 pounds so she couldn't do much.

My wife and I had been away but went down to see her as soon as we got the message. Such meetings are hard. But as we walked up to their small three room house in the woods on the hillside below our old farm, the sun shining in the yard and their black cat sitting on the steps, we felt that it would be different with Ada. It would not be that hard.

In her familiar crackling voice she gave us more details of how it happened, how his face turned blue, how quick it was, how the rescue team she'd called told her that there wasn't a thing she could have done. She told us how she and Clyde, since they were old, had talked about it. They knew it could happen anytime, and they trusted God's plan.

Ada had been a perfect partner for a man whose hard work had not earned him much money. She had made use of everything. Never threw anything away. And now, two days after his death, she had washed, sorted and repaired all his clothing—even his underwear—and had it neatly piled to give to those in their large family who could use it. Her spirit and practicality had eased our visit so much that feelings of death were nearly gone. I was already thinking I would like to have some item by which to remember Clyde when Ada remarked that I, too, just like Clyde, had begun to limp with a bad knee, and she brought me his heavy, oak cane.

It was perfect. Clyde and his cane were alike: heavy, oaken. It's too big for me when I walk with it, but it has a simple unadorned design that I like. I know it will be strong enough for any need. It stands by my back door where our dog, who spent many days with Clyde, knows whose it is. On his way out the door he stops and sniffs it carefully and wags his tail.

As it came time to leave Ada, we were close to being cheerful. But I was feeling that we needed to show something in the way of reverence or awe or sadness. Clyde was Ada's husband of 63 years and our neighbor of 15. But I couldn't think of just what to say or do. Ada now, however, spoke of the funeral plans, and they clearly met this need but in a way with which we were unaccustomed. There would be a wake Friday evening and everyone would come. The casket would be open so we could see Clyde and say goodbye. Fortunately we didn't have to respond immediately and show what was our uneasiness and discomfort with an unfamiliar ritual, because Ada continued on, telling us how the funeral home said she could take as much time to pay as she liked since she and Clyde hadn't been able to save up for the full service.

I don't know exactly what kind of people it is that have never been to an open casket wake or funeral, but my wife and I have been that kind. Our own parents, the four of them, had brief, small, and simple memorial services. Maybe too brief and simple. For the sake of Clyde and Ada, we were going to learn about something new, something uncomfortable. But something pulled us to it, and we were glad it did.

When we joined the wake at the Odd Fellows Hall a few days later we recognized about half of the many people there as friends from our small New Hampshire town. It was easy to greet each other and exchange in fairly loud voices our favorite memories of Clyde. It wasn't much different from any other party. But I did catch a glimpse of something different against the far wall of the hall. It was the coffin elevated on a platform. It was open. Ada sat in a chair near the coffin and was speaking to people lined up to approach it.

I put off thinking about this and started to talk to some of the unfamiliar people in the room. I discovered most of them were family and relatives. Clyde and Ada have 5 children, 18 grandchildren and 19 great grandchildren. All were there. They had come from as far away as Florida, most of them driving in older cars full of children and not stopping too long or expensively. The fathers were now exchanging stories of the drama of their trips, about broken fan belts, flat tires, sleeping by the roadsides.

When there were fewer people with Ada, my wife and I took the moment to approach and speak to her. She must have been saying the same things to everyone, but as she spoke she made us feel as though she had been saving up the thoughts and words just for us. She was proud and happy, she said, that everyone had made it, even down to the newest great-grandchild, just weeks old, whose family had driven straight through, overnight, from the south and had just gotten here. And, she went on, Clyde looks so peaceful and nice. Everybody says so.

I turned toward the coffin and stepped up on the platform. She kept speaking. As I brought myself to look in at Clyde, she said to be sure to see the pussy willows in his hands. She had put them there because he had given her some the first time they ever went out together. In his huge hands were a half dozen small pussy willow branches just budding out. I also saw his gold wedding band deeply embedded in his thick finger. I stood there and looked at him. Ada was still talking and telling my wife about other flower blossoms and cards that had been put in the coffin by family members.

Clyde's face did not move me, I guess, but his hands did. These were the tools that he had worked with all his life. Hard work, dirty work. I could understand what they had meant to him. And now here they were again. And it was also a part of Clyde for his hands to be clean and holding flowers and to have a ring. I began to cry. My wife stepped up and joined me. We were there but a moment, but long enough, when next Ada spoke up to us and said, "Don't forget to look in his breast pocket and see the free coupons his great grandson put there for hamburgers in case there's a McDonald's in Heaven."

# SILVER CREEK

We were still young enough, in our early 20's, to be excited with the year's first snow, and neither of us had ever seen it snow so hard. Not in the small mining village in Colorado's Rocky Mountains where Alex Cherington came from, nor I climbing in the winter Adirondack mountains of New York. We were Marine recruits marching up a narrow valley in the Sierra Pacific mountains on a winter training exercise. About 2:00 PM the flakes had started to fall heavily and in a few minutes we were scooping them up and throwing snowballs. By 3:00 it was deeper than our combat boots. The flakes had become so dense that it was impossible to see either the head or the rear of our little column of 40 men. But the two of us trudged on happily, still feeling at home and comfortable in this environment. As friends just met, we exchanged stories of our backgrounds. He, a self-taught intellectual and opera lover who had, improbably, been brought up by an pureblood Indian grandmother in a nearly abandoned mining camp, was excited to be making friends with someone who had, as he put it, "personally gone to Yale." I, in contrast, had been so romantically taken with the back country of the Colorado Rockies while climbing there in college summers that I would have eagerly changed places with him, Indian grandmother and all. By 5:00 PM it was getting dark and our column halted in a slightly broader, flat place of the valley floor.

As we waited for orders the snowfall grew almost suffocatingly thick and then, with darkness, came a silent, uncomfortable disorientation. Finally, the faint glow of a Coleman lantern up ahead, and the "word" came down from our leaders. Set up shelter-half tents, eat C rations for supper, sack out. The officers running this exercise had probably not anticipated quite these conditions, but it certainly was helping their mission to prepare us for the second winter of the Korean war.

It was not easy to set up the tents in what was now almost two feet of snow but the men all paired off and went at it. Alex and I didn't start right away. Somehow I felt like a dog who hadn't found the right place to lie down. And Alex said his grandmother's brother who had taken him camping for two summers always warned about not setting up in a narrow place or valley floor for fear a sudden thunderstorm would wash you out. We stumbled around a bit and began climbing a little way up the side of the valley. We found a big rock and a tree with a flat place by it. Perfect for both of us. We set up, ate, talked for hours, and slept, all under the relentlessly deepening but infinitely soft snow.

Being aroused from a sound sleep felt like climbing up and out of a dark hole. We heard yells and screams and the sound of a motor. We struggled to wake. The tent was pressed firmly down on us, but we could move. We couldn't tell if the voices were near or far away, but rising notes of panic, fear, and anger quickly broke us into action. We pushed up and popped the snaps that held the two shelter-halves together and shed the snow that had completely covered us. The sky was clear with the stars fading away and with the first light of dawn we were just dimly able to see. A tracked Marine Corps snow vehicle, called a Weasel, about the size of a large pickup truck, was slowly backing down over its own newly made tracks which ran in the snow up through the very center of the valley floor. Its dark red tail lights glared in the gray dawn like splashes of fresh blood. Three or four men were up and stumbling in the tracks towards the Weasel, shouting and waving their arms. It wasn't clear if they wanted the Weasel to stop or to come toward them. More men were in the tracks, down on their hands and knees inspecting what we could also now see, and with horror realized, were crushed tents and probably crushed men that had been run over by the Weasel. The snow had covered all, beautifully and deeply. In the early dawn the Weasel driver had seen nothing,...only a billowy smooth meadow of freshly fallen snow to gun his motor through on the first run of his new day.

Six months later, in Korea, when I heard that Alex Cherington had been killed on a night patrol, I had had many other vivid experiences and had made so many new friends that his death did not affect me heavily at that very time. And it might never have. It's possible that we had already enjoyed the best parts of a friendship in our three days of exchanging life stories and in our confiding of hopes and fears about Korea, then just a week ahead of us. We might never have even tried to look each other up. Like that stranger in the airport bar we've all met. Despite the intimacy you know it's all over when the planes take off. But during the next year thoughts of Alex Cherington came to me more and more often. Maybe haunted me. It was because he had died and had left his unusual, remote, and solitary story unfinished, and his grandmother alone,—with both the story and the grandmother to be remembered by possibly no one. Could it be no one? I did not want to believe that even this most simple, impoverished, and skeletal life story could just end. Without even as much as a printed period.

I wondered about Silver Creek, the little mountain town he came from, and the three room, patched-together log house he had described. I wondered if his grandmother was still alive and living there. She probably would be alone. Mostly I thought about his life, more than I thought about him. Out of the barest elements of impoverished background he had tried to put together a family story and character. He had carried this away from Silver Creek into the outside world. There was not really much in all that he had told me. Yet as he had described it and held it up for himself and for me to see, I found I could not put it down. I wanted to find and visit Silver Creek. I wanted to see his bedroom, his books, his opera records and record player. I wanted to see the schoolhouse and the elderly woman teacher who had taught him. I wanted to see his grandmother. If she were still there, I would talk to her. She would enjoy a visit, I felt sure.

Alex's story starts with his grandfather running away from home as a boy. Always a good start. The school teacher knew the story and liked to tell it to young Alex as though she had been there herself. He told it to me with probably many of her details forgotten and some new ones of his own imagination added. And my memory of what Alex told me in our tent under the snow that one night 57 years ago and what I tell you will be different. But it all did start one sunny day in Wales, where on the path to the coal mine where the grandfather and all the other boys worked, he looked off to the distance, paused for a moment, and then suddenly dropped his shovel, turned, and ran away. He ran and he ran over the hills, singing like a bird as he went, and didn't stop running until he came to a port city. There, he climbed onto a freight ship and hid, a stowaway. Your grandfather, she said, was always brave. He did what he wanted to do and what he thought was right. He didn't care what people thought. Because he sang all the time and acted so impulsively, people sometimes thought he was drunk or crazy. But he wasn't. He was just different.

One of the first different things the grandfather did after he got to Silver Creek as a miner, when the mine was still going strong before the First World War, was to take into his cabin a young, lost, Ute Indian girl. She had been left behind by her

drunken parents when they were thrown out of town for caus-
ing too much trouble. She was ten, sick, and spoke no English.
He took care of her, learned to speak her tongue, and watched
her grow. She cooked his food. She planted a garden. When she
was old enough, she became his wife. This was Alex's grandmother. But the grandmother, though loving and attentive to his
needs in the years as he grew up, would never talk about the
past. Mostly she hummed songs and spoke Indian to herself. A
daughter, Alex's mother, the only child, was born and was called
a "half breed." She spoke little Ute and less English. Early on she
was seduced by a handsome, wandering, alcoholic British war
veteran, Alex Cherington, who fathered Alex in 1931. Alex told
me, with some untypical pride, that he looked just like his father.

Nineteen thirty-one was the depth of the depression and
times were tough in Silver Creek. A fight broke out between
those miners who were willing to work for the offered lower pay
and those who would not. His grandfather was killed trying to
make peace between the sides. The teacher said Alex could be
proud of him. But his grandmother almost died of sadness. She
made an Indian doll out of her husband's red wool shirt and
kept it over the door.

As the summer clouds and sun rolled over the little mountain
valley, the grandmother's garden grew bigger and helped keep
them alive. His father and his mother helped with the work, selling a few vegetables, but they spent most of their time drinking.
When W.W.II began and London was bombed, his father, always a patriot, felt the strong call to return to England and face
the "Hun" once more. He said he was still damn-well young
enough to fight. He loudly announced he would quit booze.
Alex, who was ten, remembered these words, and said goodbye
to his father. The grandmother didn't say goodbye, but went inside and cooked a supper in which she gave Alex the extra por-
tion of meat that his father would have had, and Alex remembered this. A year later his mother left for war work in Denver,

as had other residents of Silver Creek. She sent him a Christmas card the first year she was away but after that, nothing. When the war was over, few people returned to Silver Creek. His mother was not one of them. As boys do, Alex hoped that his father, drunk or sober, would come back but he had never been heard from again. In our tent, embarrassed, Alex told me he knew it would not happen, but he still dreamed of a happy reunion.

Now living alone with his poor and reclusive grandmother in an isolated settlement, Alex gathered the wood for their fires and manure for their garden. He would put some of the manure in a cloth bag and set it to soak in a large barrel of water until "steeped". They used this strong fertilizer tea to feed the many small seedlings which were planted in old tin cans and mason jars in the big sunny window. Here they would get the critical early start needed to prosper, as no one else's did, in this mountain environment. Soon he could reach up higher than his grandmother to water the plants on the top shelf.

From the teacher he learned about books, read all of hers and all of the school's. She took him to the Gunnison Library, where, through his high school years, he spent many hours. He started reading opera librettos after hearing performances on the radio. Partly, he said, because his grandfather had been a singer and partly just because he liked it, he became a knowledgeable lover of opera. His major purchase was a record player. Opera records were hard to come by but he had a few.

One day when he came home from school there was an Indian standing in the yard. His grandmother's brother had come to find his sister. Small and wiry, but strong like his sister, he liked Alex and took him back west for two summers to the desert country where they camped and hunted. His only possessions were a Model A Ford pickup with no rear fenders and a Winchester 30-30 deer rifle. Alex learned how to use and care for both of them. The brother quietly and steadily drank Old

Crow whiskey but acted sober and was always good to Alex. Alex was 13 when the brother taught him how to drive the Ford.

One winter day the brother showed up at sunset. He was very sick. He had stomach pains and his skin was a sickly yellow. Alex, though only 15, drove him to the hospital in Gunnison. The bumpy road was painful and the brother moaned. In the empty emergency bay of the hospital Alex waited a long time, cold and frightened. Finally the doctors came and said they had operated, but the liver was so far ruined and destroyed by "roses" that they had just sewn him up again. He would die very soon. They were very sorry. Were there any other relatives who should be notified?

Alex didn't think his grandmother would go to Gunnison. He had told her that the liver was ruined and what the doctors had done and said. She had never left town, but she said she wanted to see her brother. By the next day, however, when they got back to the hospital her brother had died. The grandmother wailed and was angry with the doctors. Alex had to sign the papers that said the brother had died of "cirrhosis of the liver." When they got home he went to sleep listening to his grandmother still crying with grief. When he woke up the deer rifle was at the foot of his bed.

It is now the spring of 1953, a year after Alex's death. I am discharged from the Marine Corps, and excited again to be leaving Denver with my eyes on the high mountain ridges to the west. I would have enjoyed this trip even if I had not been looking for Silver Creek. No road map showed the town, but I knew to head for Gunnison and then to the little settlement of Old Bridge. Ask there. It was about ten miles further. I drove up the lower mountain passes and then on to Monarch Pass, at 11,312 feet, a magic place, the Continental Divide. I stopped and got out, as we had always done, almost ceremoniously, in college days crossing the high divide passes. I took long looks at our great country spread out to the East and West of me, and I felt, with pleasure and confidence, a new right to love strongly this country now that I was older and a veteran.

I got directions in Old Bridge, and only after heading up the last few miles to Silver Creek did I really begin to think about what I was going to say when I got there. I simply wanted to see the town, the house, and Alex's things—books, opera records, maybe the deer rifle. I hoped that talking to the grandmother, if she were there, would help me round out and, in a way, finish my story of Alex Cherington. And maybe I could tell her things about Alex that might make her feel proud. Or I might bring her just plain happiness in thinking that someone who had known him had come all the way up here to see her. But Alex had described her as not very talkative, and sometimes very emotional. I struggled to imagine the conversation. Since Alex and I hadn't actually served together in Korea, I could not tell her such things as "How well his men liked him" or "How well he took care of them." I had no little stories of bravery to share with her. Then I thought of the snow storm and the Weasel. I could tell it a little differently. It would be Alex alone, his thinking and efforts, that saved us. The story would be especially meaningful to her because I would emphasize not only that it was Alex's insistence that we move off the valley floor, but that it was from her brother that Alex had learned to take such precautions. I would tell her I was alive because of them. I had come here to thank her. There would be the right moment to tell her all this, particularly if she was lonely or depressed.

A homemade sign pointed down a dirt road to a cluster of about ten or fifteen buildings. There may once have been another sign above it, but this one said only "Creek." Silver was gone from the name—as it was from the mine. The buildings showed more of patched boards and plywood than of their underlying old logs. The roofs were tar paper and sheet metal, no shingles or shakes. But I was still excited to be there. The first building was the largest, with a big porch, and looked like it might be a store. I knocked and pushed the door open. Sitting at a table near me was a nice looking kid with a soda in his hands. There was a man leaning against a counter at the far end of the room. I decided to speak to the kid. I told him I used to be a friend of a Marine who had lived here whose name was Alex Cherington. I was looking for his house and maybe his grandmother, if she still lived here. The kid didn't say a word but turned his head and looked at the man. The man moved forward very slowly, looking at me, but not speaking. Finally he said, "Are you a Marine?" I told him I was, but was discharged now. Again, he did not speak right away, but I got the impression that his appraisal of me had been positive. Finally he turned to the kid and asked, "How is she?" The kid said "OK". Then the man said to the kid, "She's started to do her garden this year hasn't she?" The kid said, "Yup." The man turned to me and explained that last year she didn't do any garden. It had been pretty tough on her when the Marines came up here and told her Alex had been killed in action. The house was the one I would see if I just walked straight up the road looking at the big peak. I did, and saw that on the peak the frozen courses of snow in the couloirs and ravines, like talons of a great bird grasping the mountain, were weakening, melting with the coming of spring, and would soon be gone. Gardens would be growing. And there was the house.

The Model A Ford pickup was the clue for me. It was parked beside the house and looked like it hadn't been used for a long time. It had to be her brother's. A large rusted metal Coca-Cola advertising sign served as roofing just over the front door. I stepped up and knocked.

A voice spoke from inside. I could not quite distinguish the words, but it was an invitation to come in. She was small, dark, dressed plainly, and standing at the far end of the room by the big window. The interior was much as I had imagined. The walls were log, chinked with plaster and wadded brown newspaper. On the back wall were two doors, each probably leading to one of the bedroom additions which Alex had described. The kitchen was to the left. A couch and chairs, one an old auto seat, were on the right. Across the big window at the far end were three tiers of broad plank shelves. On them were many little seedlings and plants in a variety of containers. The sun shone in on them and on her. As the boy said, she had started the garden.

She spoke, greeting me with "Hello". Her tone was relaxed. I moved slowly toward her saying my name and saying that I had been a friend of her grandson Alex. As I moved toward her I saw the first bedroom door was closed, probably Alex's room, and the second open, showing a bed and clothes hanging on the wall. Between the doors was a table with a record player. Its top was open. I put out my hand to offer her a greeting as I approached, but at this she drew back. Her face was flat and expressionless. Now close to her I sensed the Indian. Each strand of her still black hair was as thick as straw. She stared intently at me and asked if I was a Marine like the other men. I answered by saying that Alex and I had been very good friends and had talked a lot about Silver Creek when, yes, we had been Marines together. I think she smiled. I pressed on with statements about how much I had enjoyed Alex's descriptions of his growing up here and living with her. He had told me about her garden and how much he liked to help her with it. She was warming to my overtures. But then she suddenly said, "Alex is dead." I told her that yes, I knew, they had told me also when it happened and I had been made very sad. Alex was a wonderful friend. I would have come and visited him here.

She had said a few words, agreeing with my statements, but she had not volunteered much herself and was not offering a chair or suggesting that we sit down. It was awkward and I felt that she probably did not know what to do. I decided now to tell her, as I had planned, that I wanted to thank her, to thank her and her brother for taking care of Alex and bringing him up, because he had saved my life. Suddenly, as I spoke, she looked around the room, then at me, and said, "He saved your life. You are here, Alex is dead." I had imagined telling her the story carefully, emphasizing the parts that would warm her. But to counter what was clearly her rising emotion, turning to anger, I was forced to blurt out just the most important parts, hoping that she would sense my appreciation of Alex and my debt to him. I had come here to thank him by thanking her. And her brother. But it was not working.

As I mumbled, feeling desperate and foolish, she turned away from me towards the big window and the trays of seedlings in the sun. She repeated, "Alex is killed. Gone. It is all gone." She reached out and put her hand beside a tray of small green sprouting seedlings, held it there for a moment, and then, with rising vehemence, said, " Gone. Everything spoiled, all ruined." and swept the tray of seedlings off onto the floor. "Killed, killed," she said and pushed another tray back over the edge of the plank. She was crying and trying to tip up the whole plank when, reaching toward her, I cried, "No, no, don't." She turned and said, "You are alive. Alex is dead. He's killed."

I didn't prevent her from tumbling all the containers off the planks. There was the loud crash of breaking glass as they hit the floor. "Killed," she yelled. "Everything is ruined. Go away," she yelled louder, "Go away."

I did. I ran from a house filled solid with despair. I held my arms bent over my head for protection from above. I was too ashamed to stop at the store. I got in the car and took off. An hour later, on my way back to somewhere, going over Monarch Pass, I did not stop to get out and look again proudly at my great country.

# OLD HARTFORD

A stronger man than I, a man with more integrity, would not have allowed it. He would have insisted that he had been born in Wallingford, or Springfield, or wherever it was he had been born. In my case, California. And I did say it—Pasadena, California— at least twice. But in truth no such place would have been accepted; certainly not naming nearby East Hartford and probably not even now socially acceptable West Hartford. Clearly, from the very beginning it was going to be Hartford. And it was Hartford. Reading aloud what he had written, this determined author said the words over again slowly, with evident pleasure, and in a way that invited me to join him in that pleasure. "Yes, now—'Walter N. Morrison, a native of Hartford, —'"

Lyman Brainerd, President of The Hartford Steam Boiler Inspection and Insurance Company, was writing a press release to appear in *The Hartford Courant* the next day which would announce the election of Walter Morrison, me, to be an officer of the Company. I was proud and excited. I was also easy game for the gentlemanly manipulations of a skilled operator. Mr. Brainerd, or LBB as I think of him, had used the car salesman's technique of getting me to say "yes" to a series of pleasant questions before presenting the hard one that he knew I would not want to say "yes" to. I had gone to school at Andover? "Yes." And you served our country in the Marine Corps? "Yes." And then after your military service you went down to New Haven for your college, that is, to Yale? "Yes, sir, that's right." Finally, the last question. I didn't see it coming, but I know I corrected him at least once. Yet despite my attempts at correction, the very first sentence in *The Hartford Courant* article the next morning began "Walter N. Morrison, a native of Hartford...."

Old Hartford was not to be denied. Even my father, who had once enrolled me in an exclusive club of third generation native Californians, did not grumble over this "little mistake" when he called to congratulate me on reading the paper the next day. He, too, had been bought by the cultural power of this old-rich city on the banks of the Connecticut River.

If this does not sound possible, or true, that such a little thing as where an officer in his company was born could be so important as to merit a printed deception, consider this one. Carolyn Taylor, my father-in-law's older sister, the spry and sparrow-like necessary spinster aunt for all occasions of family gathering, lived in an apartment on Prospect Avenue. Prospect divides Hartford from West Hartford, with the east side of the street being in Hartford and the west side being in the town of West Hartford, a different place. I know my geography and maps well enough, and I know how to read a compass well enough to know with certainty that Aunt Star, as she was called, lived on the west side of the street, West Hartford. But she didn't. She lived in Hartford. I discovered this because she told me so.

I had stopped by one snowy December evening about a week before Christmas to pay her a call on my way home from work. There was always a glass of sherry to be enjoyed and some easy conversation emanating from her skillfully lived long life of delightful sociability. On this evening she had mentioned, with a strong note of disapproval, that a friend had recently moved to West Hartford. I quickly reminded her that she, herself, lived in West Hartford. She said that no, she would not live in West Hartford, only new people lived there. Mark Twain had lived just a few blocks down in Hartford near her, and they had shared the same doctor for many years. She lived in Hartford. To present the necessary compelling documentary evidence in support of her assertion she teetered toward me, slowly, with the decanter of sherry in one hand and a clutch of a dozen newly received Christmas cards in the other. "See," she said, " they are all addressed to me in Hartford, Prospect Avenue, Hartford. Not West Hartford". And they were. That postman had no more integrity than I.

There is a power in assertion, in belief, that is sometimes missing in rationality. Such power carried Aunt Star to the age of 103 in her Hartford, Old Hartford, apartment where she died. One of her friends there for a number of years was Madam Marguerite Yourcenar, renowned intellectual, author of many books, and the first woman to be elected to the French Academy of Letters. That this woman also succumbed to, or at least enjoyed, the unrealities, the myths and the absurdities of Old Hartford and its dwindling practitioners has always helped me feel less guilty about selling my western birthright for a position in the business world and the society of a city coasting inexorably downhill. As I left Lyman Brainerd's office after accepting his text of the press release, I should have emulated Galileo and muttered under my breath "Nevertheless, I was born in Pasadena."

There is a scholarly book waiting to be written about the decline of Old Hartford. While I am sure there is an Old Manchester and an Old Fall River, maybe even an Old Sheyboygan, with decaying empty factories like Colt's Firearms or Underwood Typewriter, and businesses like Aetna Life that have lost their profitability if not their buildings, it cannot be the same as Old Hartford. The compelling documentary evidence, in this case, is that in 1870 Hartford was the single richest city in the nation and by 2000, 130 years later, it was the poorest. (New York Times, August 26, 2002) In her 103 years, Carolyn Taylor had enjoyed its glory days and then saw the greatest descent experienced by any American city, not to imply that she herself noticed. In fact, it was partly because they, the Carolyn Taylors and the Lyman Brainerds, didn't notice or understand the changes going on about them, even when the city burned—more later —, that makes their words and their lives ironic and humorous, and in the end endearing.

Though I was not always there, Hartford was my home where I lived and worked for sixty years, the last and probably the steepest years of its great decline. At one time, 1944, I worked for The Merrow Machine Company, the last manufacturing plant with the tenacity to survive in a city which no longer cared for factories and offered no help, and later I worked for 29 years for the Hartford Steam Boiler, the last Hartford insurance company to lose its independence and be merged into a larger New York City company. This is some of what I saw.

Picture a visiting business man from Texas. He is a Ph.D. in chemical engineering, young, smart, and big, like his state. He is good-natured and curious, and very proud of Radian, the new engineering consulting business he has founded. Don Carlton thrives on newness and change. He and Jack Washburn meet on the Steam Boiler Board of Directors and they like each other. Jack has now succeeded his father as President of Merrow Machine and invites Don to come on over and see the plant— he'll get a kick out of it. I tag along for the nostalgia of seeing my old work place.

The factory building is three stories tall and the heavy boxes of metal parts for their product, industrial sewing machines, have to be carried up and down stairs in an old time elevator. The longest production line, if it really is one, seems to be about twenty feet long. The sewing machine itself is a model unchanged for decades and is perhaps one of the most complex, finely-built pieces of early industrial machinery to be found. Sometimes the factory runs at a pace that takes a full year for some of the most critical parts to be completed. Don is amazed.

He looks at a Cincinnati milling machine. It's almost 100 years old. It has a three digit serial number. We all enjoy the tour.

Returning to Jack's office for a final few minutes, I notice that Don has stopped listening to the conversation and is staring at a framed document on the wall. "Oh," says Jack, "that's just an old patent." "But," exclaims Don, "it's signed by John Quincy Adams and James Monroe. Texas wasn't even a state then."

We stand up to leave, but Jack stops us at a door in the hall and says we have to take a quick look at the office where design work is done. His father, in fact, is working on plans for a new machine. Jack opens the door and we see an elderly man at a high slant-top desk covered with protractors, T squares, paper and pencils. The elderly man, bending over the work, does not notice us. He is lost in thought. He is taking a nap.

On the sidewalk, in front of the factory on Laurel Street, Don Carlton looks up at its solid old brick structure and says, "Jack, my friend, if there were anything like this in Texas, the whole thing would be in a museum. You could quit working and make good money just by charging admission." Jack thinks about asking Carlton to join Merrow's Board of Directors.

But Radian and Don Carlton showed up and became part of the Hartford Steam Boiler only near the end of the story when Bill Wilde, its new president, was trying hard to bring HSB into the twentieth century before the twenty-first started. When I began with the company in the late 1950's HSB was a publicly owned stockholder insurance company with inspectors and salesmen in every state of the nation. But it didn't have air conditioning in its home office, a formal pension plan, or health insurance for its employees that included pregnancy. Pregnancy was considered a "self-inflicted" condition. Sarah Taylor, my wife, was pregnant.

In a great many ways the company reflected the character and values of its president, Lyman B. Brainerd, whose father had been president some years before him. Lyman himself was a trim, medium-sized man, always impeccably but inconspicuously dressed. He moved with a careful sprightliness. When younger, he had flown his own plane and was well known, if not notorious, for landing on golf course fairways to catch the party or play a few rounds. It is said he was forced to abandon Yale after too much partying. It may not be true, but with admiration I repeat it anyway. I do know he graduated from Trinity. He had blue eyes and engaging expressions on his face. In the company of friends he was lively and humorous, but reserved in public. On a few very hot July or August days days he would remove his suit jacket at work. The word would spread quickly through out the home office and only then would we all feel safe in taking off our jackets.

Lyman Brainerd knew and trusted the Hartford men he had selected for ushers at his wedding. Thus, in fulfilling an important corporate duty, he selected a number of them as Directors of "his" publicly owned Company. You can pay a consulting firm a lot of money to come up with weaker criteria. Later, but still some years before his retirement, he graciously asked Bill Wilde and me for our input about directors so we wouldn't be saddled with just his old cronies. Rare, gentlemanly behavior. Jack Washburn had been an usher at Bill's wedding and Joel Alvord, the rare useful banker, was a fishing buddy of mine. Was old Hartford starting to replicate itself?

Though HSB had what was called a "Stockholder Audit Committee" (both of its two members, George Gilman and Henry Moses, had been ushers), this committee's sole responsibility was to supervise an annual count of the securities in our vault. When audit committees with broad powers over all aspects of honesty and accuracy throughout the Company became standard, LBB would have absolutely none of it. He felt that if you subjected a person to audit you were implying that he might well be dishonest. He would not make that implication of his employees. There was something in my background of leading troops that agreed with this. As Treasurer, I eventually had to capitulate and establish such a committee, but I staffed it with people who patently could not be suspected of thinking ill of anyone. One of them was Tom Martyn, whose grandfather, Frank Cheney, of silk fame, had been an early director of the Company. Of course.

Annual reports were mailed to the list of our existing stockholders routinely for the first 100 years or so, and when eventually we were pressured to do it, we mailed quarterly reports to those same stockholders. But we would not mail any reports to "outsiders", people who were not stockholders. We would not give financial information to the newspapers. It was not their company so there was no obligation to communicate with them. As we debated the issue, I was reminded of a moment with Caroline Taylor. She had been informed that she was to be congratulated on her 100th birthday by Bob Steele, Hartford's much loved radio commentator. Her startled reaction was of horror, and she said, "Then my name will be on every shop girl's lips." I think LBB's aversion to giving our reports to the newspapers was a masculine version of this same Old Hartford distaste for publicity.

But there was irony here, too. LBB was secretly chairman of the board of trustees that controlled *The Hartford Courant*, the nation's oldest continuously published newspaper. One might have thought he would have liked a little copy for his paper. I say secretly because his name could never be found on any masthead or other document and no one I ever spoke to seemed to know it. It became important and I discovered it when large newspaper chains tried to buy the Courant. Lyman likewise was chairman of the Trinity College trustees, but this fact appeared on no public document or college catalogue. Can you imagine the frustration of the students that night in the late 1960s when they corralled the trustees in a building and demanded to talk to the chairman but couldn't figure out who he was? The next morning you couldn't tell from his looks that Lyman Brainerd had sat on a darkened hallway floor all night listening to students scream obscenities. At about 10:30 AM at work he did, however, mention it. And then we went on to discuss the possible usefulness of computers in the Insurance industry, or was it the shed for employees' bicycles?

In Afghanistan for more than 100 years the British and the Russians played what was called The Great Game, fighting for influence at this old crossroads. But no profit they ever made equaled that of Old Hartford's life insurance companies in their first 100 years or so playing their great game. Get everybody to give you their money and hold it invested until they die. There will be far more than enough to finally pay death claims and along the way some paltry dividends to policy holders or stockholders. Don't tell anybody about this, and specifically don't report any more money as earnings than you absolutely have to. Reported earnings are subject to taxation and will also attract the attention of outsiders who might want in on the game. Don't split your stock until you absolutely have to. (Just before bursting, Travelers did this with a 25 for 1 split.) The most foolish act of all would be to call the capital gains from the investment portfolio "income". So money began to pile up in great heaps around town and was added to from the sale of shade-grown cigar wrapper tobacco, typewriters, and Colt 45 pistols. Everybody was rich, though few showed it and some didn't even know it, and during the Great Depression not even the least employee got laid off.

But over the years many people around the country began to want other things from their money than saving it for their death, and Hartford was slow to realize this. Also, those damned outside auditors began messing with the financial statements. John Bertoud of Coopers & Lybrand had the job of telling Lyman Brainerd that capital gains were income. The Feds were already taxing the gains and most other companies in town had abandoned principle and capitulated on this reporting issue, but HSB had more gains than most. The meeting was long. As we sat around the great four inch thick wooden conference table—made by the Taylor Lumber Company—Coopers added the additional complaint that we had set aside as reserves too much money for unsettled claims. We were understating our net income. For Lyman, considering capital gains as income was really a moral issue, akin to the sin of spending principal, and the color began to rise above his white collar. For me, over-reserving for claims was simply avoiding too big a rise in earnings this year that might be hard to equal the next year. We were polite, but adamant. Coopers explained that if we didn't comply, they would not be able to give us a "clean" certificate and they would have to record an exception in their report on our figures. Each side repeated their arguments, but to no avail. Finally, Lyman Brainerd was impolite for the only time I ever knew about and he said, " Well then, I am sorry, but it appears that this year we will just have to do without the letter from your trade union." There was a long and uneasy silence, duly absorbed by the old wooden table. Lyman got up and left. It has occurred to me, on reflection, that maybe he wasn't impolite. It's possible he thought they were a trade union. Anyway, our Old Hartford Company was in trouble 30 or 40 years ago for understating earnings. Have you ever heard of that happening anywhere else, or recently?

Harold Geneen, head of International Telephone and Telegraph, was the first truly dangerous man to spot the piles of moldering money in Hartford and set deliberate plans for it. He had put together a string of twenty consecutive quarters of increasing earnings at ITT and his stock had soared. He enjoyed this and wanted to keep it up. He spotted $500 million of unrealized and unreported capital gains at the Hartford Fire Insurance Company and figured that that would keep him going for awhile. Using his highly valued—maybe overvalued—ITT stock he could offer a lot for undervalued Hartford Fire stock. After he promised not to fire any employees or move the company out of Hartford, to continue to make local charitable contributions, and to gain the approval of both the Insurance Commissioner and the heads of the other insurance companies that held stock in Hartford Fire, everybody agreed to the acquisition. There were financial incentives for some executives, common today, not then. The smallest and last insurance company whose president he wished would vote for the deal was HSB and Lyman Brainerd, and of course (you already know) he wouldn't. Harold Geneen was not from Hartford, and he wasn't even an insurance man. If this was a snobby way of dismissing the man, Brainerd had absolutely unerring savvy about who was a raider. We had been wooed by several ourselves and had so far successfully put them off. (Did the suitor know how terribly devastating a large boiler explosion could be, how completely unpredictable, maybe even blowing tomorrow, and perhaps in a school or hospital? We didn't mention our reinsurance.) And Geneen was a raider. He was also sufficiently determined to meet Brainerd, who had declined all invitations, that he had his team almost literally trap Brainerd in a parking garage where Geneen was stationed with his hand extended for a handshake. Brainerd, caught off guard, shook it. He came back to the office disconsolate and anxious to wash his hands.

### $100,000,000 dollars for sale, cheap
### Buy it for only $70,000,000

Walking back from lunch at the The Hartford Club past the ground floor window of Lyman Brainerd's office, I called his attention to this sign which my assistant had placed in the window while we were eating. Our stock was selling at a 30% discount to its liquidating value. After some heavy thought, Lyman finally acknowledged with a smile that his conservative financial policies which had made the company so strong were now making us vulnerable. He had a good sense of humor. We started rapidly increasing the dividend and got the board to approve buying in our own stock. But another hard one for him to believe a little later was that The Aetna Life was secretly buying up our stock as part of an acquisition program. Olcott Smith was Chairman of the Aetna, and he was Lyman's brother-in-law. Was Old Hartford coming apart? In defense, we bought a block of 10% of our stock from a West Coast mutual fund just minutes before it was to be sold to the Aetna. To top Aetna's bid the fund made us pay $3 a share above the market price. Frank Stevenson and Frank Chapman and other lawyers meeting in my office told us that the Securities and Exchange Commission and stockholders who were not getting a chance to sell their stock at such a nice premium would have a real complaint and we should not do this. Brainerd gave me a wink and an imperceptible nod, got up and, leading the others out of my office, closed the door behind him, leaving me alone. I figured he expected me to land the plane on the fairway. I placed the phone call and bought the stock. I did get a letter of complaint, which I should have saved. Just one letter. It was perfectly written, laying out all the reasons why such a purchase should not have been made and indicating that the writer would shut up if I offered him an even higher price for his stock. Blackmail! It was good friend and senior old Hartford National Bank officer, Tom Sargent, Joe's father.

I should have saved another letter I got about this time. In reward for his courage in holding the sign in the window, Maurice Slayton, my assistant, had been named an officer by Mr. Brainerd. I forget how we handled his Vermont birth, but it was up to me to write the letter recommending him for the customary membership in the Hartford Club, which I did. To my great surprise, my thoughtful and laudatory letter was returned as inadequate. The Club's membership secretary, Joe Proctor, had written me to say that he had received my fulsome letter, but that I had failed to state whether or not Mr. Slayton was a gentleman. In reply, I wrote a one sentence letter, "Mr. Slayton is a gentleman." and dated it a century earlier, 1870. Did he notice? He accepted Moe Slayton.

Moe picked some good stocks for us in those early days. But many of his best recommendations were turned down by our investment committee which was unfortunately composed of some of our oldest directors. In one meeting they turned down, in order, Texas Instruments, Tampax and American Express. That they turned down the first two was disappointing yet not surprising, but I thought American Express would be perfect. Moe described how the Company's new invention, a plastic credit card, would make travel much easier for many more people. After a few "Harrumphs", James L. Thomson, Lindsay's father, said "No." There were already entirely too many people traveling, and this new idea was bound to make things worse. He was leaving the next week on his annual trip to Bermuda which, with effort, he was still able to enjoy despite the island's now allowing motor cars.

If Joe Proctor and James L.Thomson were simply examples of old men who had failed to keep up with the pace of change, Lyman Brainerd's response to the proposal that HSB institute stock options for its officers deserves more thought. By the early 1970s most of the stock insurance companies in Hartford had started such programs. We felt pressed to consider the idea. I had assembled all the articles and studies on the subject and they all recommended stock options. It was just a matter of how many, for whom, and how to do it in a way that gave officers the greatest incentive to perform. It was another long meeting around the big table. Though we all had many questions, I can remember only one specific question that Lyman asked. Would the officers who set the amount of reserves needed for claims that had not yet been settled get stock options? The answer seemed to be yes, it would be hard to exclude them. The conversation slowly wound down and we waited for some summary or conclusion from Lyman. As if he were speaking of eight year-old boys tying firecrackers on the tails of dogs, he said one word, "Mischievous. I think stock options are mischievous." Today, we know they are. And while I am not sure they were the undoing of Old Hartford, they haven't done much to build a new Hartford.

Most people realized that old Hartford was no longer serene and comfortable but was under attack on that night in September 1969 when the the big chain grocery store in the north end of town was set on fire by rampaging mobs of unhappy people. This was part of a national malaise at the time, but Hartford had its particular problems,too. There were no more factory or manufacturing jobs in town for people with limited education and there were a lot of such people living there partly because Puerto Ricans and others were flown in on one-way tickets during the summer to work in Connecticut's tobacco fields and then left to survive on the city's strained welfare budget in the winter. They didn't speak English so they didn't go to school. So the city burned. It wasn't as bad as Watts but it sure changed the feel of Old Hartford.

I stopped at Aunt Star's on my way home from work. I needed a peaceful moment away, far away, from the tensions of work and the city's problems. I got it. We had chatted about the headlines in the paper only briefly, but into my second sherry I asked this old gal who had seen so much of Hartford's history unfold what she thought might be the reason they were burning down buildings in the city. "Well," she said, "I think it's because all of our good young men are now going down to New Haven for College instead of staying here in Hartford at Trinity."

# IN BANGOR

There was one name from New England. Of all the men in my old platoon, only one now lived in New England. According to the roster they'd sent me, Marines head Southwest to retire, to Texas, to Oklahoma, three in Missouri. Most of the names I didn't remember. Fifty years ago in Korea they'd meant a lot. But some were familiar. As I slowly reread the list, memories of faces and voices came back. Norman Leblanc was definitely one I recalled, and he lived in Bangor, Maine, 72 Pine Street.

I wanted to go. I've had no contact with Marines, haven't sought any, but how could you miss with a guy from Bangor? He might be a logger, as I was once, or a fisherman. And by the time I called him, my memory had taken shape. He was young, like most of the men in the platoon, really just a big boy. He was husky, a little rambunctious, and humorous. He was a good Marine and on one occasion, if my memory was right, had shown some valuable back country smarts. On the phone, he remembered me almost immediately. He said he would be right there at his house anytime I got there.

As I drove east on route 25, through Ossipee, Kezar Falls, and Standish, toward Portland and Bangor, I was thinking about never having met with a veteran's group or gone to a reunion when I saw on the outskirts of a little town one of those sad and lonely buildings, with an empty parking lot, the Lodge building of the American Legion or the Veterans of Foreign Wars. They are usually located out where the real estate isn't too expensive, not far from the highway department's gravel pit and maintenance sheds. I've noticed them for years, and wondered. They can look proud if the sun is shining on fresh paint, but usually they look sad and old. In the twilight, as the windows darken, could you slip in and hear the stories starting up again? Stories which must have been told now for many, many years. Would you hear, "at Belleau Wood," or "one time at Chateau Thierry?" or would they not start until, "so you were at Guadalcanal?" or, "tank mechanic, North Africa". These stories would now mostly be just ghosts in the rafters, but on Friday and Saturday nights living men would be there having a beer and talking of the Chosin Reservoir or the Tet offensive. They would be looking each other in the eye, dead level, and know they were friends who understood each other. No one else there to think they were boasting, or complaining. Just telling their stories, some simple, some tough.

In December of 1951, our platoon was holding a high mountain ridge on the eastern sector of the front line. There was not much action. Sometimes we would be ordered to go into wild country back behind the lines to mop up any enemy that had hidden out during our last advance. I was the platoon leader but would take just one of the three squads. These patrols were not very dangerous, but they were long hikes in rough terrain and deep snow carrying weapons and ammunition. One time as we were working up a valley we became aware that the woods were thinning ahead of us and there was a cluster of a half a dozen small houses. We spread out and approached slowly, watching the houses carefully. The little village appeared to be completely deserted. There was no smoke from any chimney and there were no tracks visible in the fresh snow.

I was about to give the order for some of the men to advance when Norman, kneeling behind me said, "Sir, there's one house with icicles hanging on the eaves. Just that one. Over on the left. It's been heated. Somebody's probably in there." We fired a shot in the air to see what happened. In about 30 seconds three men with rifles ran out the other side of the house and into the woods behind. They were in dark clothes, not the white quilted cotton of the Chinese who opposed us on the front at this time. They could have been North Korean soldiers or just plain back country locals who were trying to live there. Maybe it had been their home.

We didn't succeed in capturing these guys but we did complete the rest of our orders. Up in these mountains the houses were wooden board construction, quite pretty, not the adobe or mortar of the valleys. We set them on fire and burnt them down. Deny any enemy their shelter, but most of us didn't like doing it.

As I headed into Bangor, I was remembering this patrol, but I had also in mind other occasions and events that I believed Norman and I had shared and could talk about. I even had a photo of him and his squad during that Marine Corps religious ceremony of rifle inspection. It showed him with an almost illegally big smile while I checked the bore of his Browning Automatic Rifle.

Though I have seen "new" Bangor with its malls and motels out on the edge of town where I-95 passes by, I had not been into the old part of town for many years. The residential areas just off the main streets as I headed for the center of town and 72 Pine Street looked old. There were two and three-family houses, tall, of the sort built more than 100 years ago. I felt as if I were stepping back into an old, earlier American world. Yes, there would be fishermen and loggers living here. Some factory workers. I knew what they would look like, and how they would speak, and I would be comfortable with them. And I was right, but for one surprise.

Norman and I had both been visualizing each other as 18 and 24 year olds. We got some laughs out of this, but there were still impediments to familiarity. He seemed "old school", deferential. He was retired from the chicken business, another big Maine industry. He and his wife, he told me, and some remaining children and some grandchildren, lived on the ground floor of this big, old two-family house. He led me in to the main room with a large round table covered with books, coffee cups, newspapers, pads and pencils, shopping bags, a package of diapers and a plate of doughnuts. Obviously I was at the operations center of a big, multigenerational family. Though I was aware there were other people in the building, we sat down alone at the big table. Norman said, pointing to it, "Sir, that's the best chair. Why don't you sit there." He had said "sir" a couple of times. I said, "Hey, Norman, we're both nothing but a couple of old grandfathers now, don't call me 'Sir' any more. OK? Call me Wally." "OK," he said, but it was hard for him. I don't think he got "Wally" out of his mouth once, really. He just stopped calling me anything. I understood, and I didn't press him. We were going to have fun anyway.

The picture got us going. We began to put the names on the others in the picture and tell stories of what we remembered about them. Norman also had not kept up with any of the other men after he had left the Corps. So we two equally isolated veterans at the far edges of the Marine Corps world, northern New England, began together for the first time to recreate the most vivid world we had ever lived in, a world now fifty years gone and on the other side of the world. We warmed to the job and soon became almost scared at how strongly our similar memories, which had lived each quietly alone in our separate heads, came flooding back to join each other.

But for me the biggest surprise came when suddenly in through the front door and straight for our table breezed a young man carrying school books and a laptop computer. He was well dressed in brightly colored athletic clothes in strong contrast to the age and darkness of the house and old Bangor surroundings. As he put his armload down on the far side of the table, he looked at Norman and said, "Hi, Grandfather, good afternoon." There was more than the average note of respect in his address. I was puzzled, but felt a shot of pride for Norman go through me. This boy, who was calling Norman "Grandfather", was Chinese. A very handsome, young, clear eyed Chinese. If Botticelli had drawn Chinese they would have looked like this boy.

"Sir," said Norman, addressing me and standing up, "This is Nicholas. He is engaged to marry my granddaughter as soon as they graduate next spring." I reached over and shook Nicholas's hand and said that I was an old Marine Corps friend of Norman's and had just stopped by to say Hello. He asked if I had been in Korea with Norman.

"Yes," I said. "We have been having fun talking over old memories." I continued to be impressed with the bright, young looks of this person and enjoyed the message of respect that he seemed to give me as well as Norman.

"Grandfather has shown us his war medals and his honorable discharge from the Marine Corps, but he doesn't tell us very much. It must be a pleasure to talk to you."

Norman explained that Nicholas was going to get a degree in computer science because that's where the best jobs were. Nicholas said that he was good at math and liked computer games, so he figured computer science would be half way between those two. We laughed, and Nicholas went into the kitchen to get something to eat.

Norman said, quietly, "He's a real good kid. The smartest guy in his class. I think my granddaughter is real lucky."

"I agree with you," I said. "And he's the best looking and politest kid I've met in a long time."

Norman explained he was glad somebody in the family was going to be in one of these new fields because the chicken and egg business was going downhill in Maine. One of his own sons was a logger, working for Great Northern in Millinocket and that wasn't too great a life anymore, either. Nicholas had sort of perked up the whole family and everybody liked him. Nicholas came back with a Coke, sat down with his lap top on the far side of the table, opened some books and went quietly and intently to work.

I told Norman I had started out as a logger. He liked that, relaxed some more, and then he started telling me his memory of another event. On the coldest night of the winter while we were still on our hill, he had led a couple of our guys on a raid to break into a nearby army supply truck. They were after the Army's new "Mickey Mouse" insulated boots which the Marines didn't have yet. He said the other guys were afraid I would make them take the boots back, but he said he had been sure I wouldn't. He remembered that at inspection the next morning he appealed to me with the strongest look he could put in his eyes. He got a steady look back, and wasn't sure what it meant, but I had asked no questions.

Then Norman said one of the times with me he remembered best was the morning we "captured" the Chinese prisoner. Just after dawn, I had been making one of my regular checks of each of the foxholes—we called them hooches—on our part of the line. I had stopped at his hooch and was having a smoke and talking with him and his buddy, all of us sitting on the edge of the parapet. Simultaneously we all became aware that there was a Chinese soldier standing absolutely immobile about 75 feet downhill from us just at the edge of the woods. Somehow, none of us had seen him in his white quilted suit. His hat and his shoulders were covered deeply with the fresh light snow of the night before. His arms were in the surrender position. He had crept up in the dark, undetected, and stood there, patiently immobile for an hour or two, waiting for dawn and someone to accept his surrender.

Norman continued to tell the story and was exclaiming about how tough Chinese feet must be, because, like this guy, all they ever had to keep them warm in the winter was straw and rags to wrap around their flimsy pink rubber-soled summer sneakers when suddenly, in a voice that startled us both, he was interrupted from across the table.

"Grandfather, you never told me you fought Chinese people." The face was no longer Botticelli. Hurt and anger and surprise were there and in the voice.

"No, I never did," Norman said very slowly, his animation and excitement gone. He turned his head toward me, lowered it, and looked me in the eyes with a request, an appeal.

I was trying for words, but before they came, my own memory of the "Mickey Mouse" boot scene flashed instantly back to me. Norman, with his fire team. Four of them in the big black boots standing just off the ridge line with the north wind blowing hard dry snow over the ground and swirling around the boots. Rifle inspection. But my mind was racing on the boots. Brand new shiny black insulated army boots. Stolen. Must have been stolen last night. If the army shows up and asks the Captain, these boys are in trouble. Norman is looking at me. Smiling, conspiratorial, pleading, but just a little bit. Mostly he's trusting. He's a kid. He trusts me. And I know that without question he would do anything I might have to ask him to. While I struggle I give him no clue. I inspect the rifles, all perfect. I think to myself, these guys have done what they're supposed to do. So will I. I'll protect their ass. I'll tell the Captain so he'll be prepared, and tell him I gave the boys the OK to try last night. I yell into the wind, "Dismissed."

Norman is still now looking at me, and Nicholas knows I have been thinking, when I say, "Nicholas, your grandfather here never shot at any Chinese. While we were on that hill he's talking about there wasn't any shooting."

"But I can remember being told that some U.S. soldiers tried to invade China across a river and the Chinese people had to fight them back. A lot were killed."

"Norman and I weren't there for that battle, but some Chinese Army soldiers did later attack down into Korea and came to our defense line. That's who we saw." I could tell the boy was still hurting. This tough moment, the result of my visit, was perhaps the closest he had ever come to war, to even thinking about it, and what "grandfather" might have done.

Almost crying, I thought, Nicholas then blurted out, "And you were laughing, laughing about the Chinese soldier not having anything but rags and grass to keep his feet warm."

We were getting deeper, and I wasn't turning his feelings around. Maybe he had thought about this, maybe he knew a lot, but had suppressed his feelings, and now they were breaking through. Norman looked terrible. His head hung down and his hands were clenched in his lap. For the first time I saw him as an old man, like myself, but for only a moment.

"Nicholas," I said, "Let me tell you about the kinds of things my buddy here, grandfather, did in Korea. One time, following orders to level a village we were burning down all the houses. Suddenly, your grandfather, Norman, stepped forward in front of us all and stopped us and called out loudly 'don't torch that house over there, I think there are people in it,' and it turned out he was right. There were three people in it. The other guys would have just burnt everything down."

"So how did you know?" Nicholas shot quickly back to Norman. His failure to include the address 'grandfather' was conspicuous, but I felt he was maybe ready to buy some new thoughts. If only the memory I had carried with me for 50 years was right and still in Norman's head, too.

"Tell him, Norman." I said.

Norman, raising his head, but not yet looking at Nicholas, said. "Icicles. There were icicles hanging off the roof."

"So? How does that prove anything?" Nicholas, the boy from the computer generation and virtual reality, was interested.

Norman sat up, grew younger and spoke more warmly. "Well, you don't see it so much anymore, roofs being insulated now, but I learned about it from my father when I was kid going with him on his work. The way he made his living in those hard times was to buy groceries here in Bangor and then drive them out into the back country, especially in winter, to sell them to poor farmers and wood cutters, living in little old board shacks, who couldn't get into town, didn't have a car or money for gas. Sometimes we would push through deep snow bringing a loaf of bread and a couple of cans of beans to some old guy or a grandmother, or maybe even a family with kids, and they couldn't pay."

"I still don't understand what icicles have to do with all this," Nicholas interrupted.

"Wait, you will. My father mostly would leave the food with them anyway and say something about next summer when they got work again they could pay him then. This was hard on my father, because my mother would be waiting for the money to buy our own groceries and he would have to explain. But it wasn't as bad as something else. A house with no icicles."

"Whenever we'd approach a house my father would quickly look to see if there were fresh icicles. As soon as he saw them he would always say, 'well, that's good. They've still got heat and are alive in there.' Icicles mean heat inside. A couple of times I helped him to bring in wood and light a fire for old people who were near frozen. It was scary for me. I got so I was looking for the icicles even before he did. Before I was old enough to go with him I think he did find some people who had frozen. It was a hard job in those days, the depression. He didn't talk about it much. He was always just glad to see icicles."

They were looking at each other. There was a long silent moment before Nicholas said, "Grandfather, why don't you please ever tell us about what you did in the old days?"

I was breathing easier again and felt we were back on safe ground. Norman didn't get to try an answer for this last question because his wife now stepped in from the kitchen with cups of coffee and a scold for Norman for not having already offered me something. Nicholas defended him.

Later that afternoon, heading west back home, I was blinded by the sun setting over the Ossipee Range shining directly in my eyes. I came to the town with the Legion Hall on the outskirts and I pulled into the empty parking lot. I sat and rested and watched the yellow of the sun's warmth slowly leave the building's face. If someone were to come, I thought, I would go inside and put my story up in the rafters with the rest.

# MEN AND DOGS AND THE DANBURY FARM

In the beginning days at the Danbury farm, while we were digging out old wells and rebuilding stone walls, my helper, Alan Brownell, would often tell me that his earliest childhood memories were of being forced to go bear hunting with his father. Despite frequent and impassioned tellings I could never quite figure out if young Alan was actually bait, to lure the bears, or was he used by his father as a dog to run ahead through the woods rousting out sleepy bears so the old man could come along and shoot them. In either case Alan did not love his father for this practice but he was now proud of it. He had become a skilled backwoodsman himself and had a reputation as a strong tough guy nobody messed with. Despite his modest size Alan policed some of the town's improperly drunk young toughs with his own fists because he thought the law was too slow, and he told the state highway department that if they let the big trucks full of Boston's trash run their route through Danbury center he would shoot each one's tires out while hiding in ambush. Some improper drunkenness continues even to this day in Danbury, but the trucks never came.

Sarah discovered first that Alan was not entirely what he seemed, though he mostly was. His blue eyes and good looks had attracted her, and soon she had him telling her about Evelyn who lived with him in his homemade log cabin. One wanted to know about Evelyn. She did not come from Danbury, or any place nearby. She came from Puerto Rico and was a gorgeous young woman. Seeing her around old Danbury was like spotting a fresh blooming rose in late November's dying grass. This illusion was not at all weakened by the vivid tattoos always visible on her vibrant bare brown arms or by noticing the loaded 38 special Smith and Wesson revolver she kept on the seat beside her in the car when she came to pick Alan up from work. She entered my fantasy world, pistol in hand, before I even knew her name.

Their story goes like this. Along with a half dozen buddies getting properly drunk, Alan and his widely-known dog Beaufort, a well muscled, brown, short-haired "Blue Tick" hound with Jersey cow mascara-outlined eyes, had been sitting on "hippie hill", Danbury's small but best known gathering place close by the road in the center of town. A beautiful dark-skinned young woman stopped her car and got out to ask directions. As she began to unfold a map of Vermont, Alan offered to help. It took a new map, a shared cold beer, and about 30 minutes before he was sure she now knew how to find the address she had shown him in the Bronx, New York. Before she left, he learned that her black husband had recently died of a drug overdose, she had had to send her three young children back to Puerto Rico, and was now heading for her sister's house where she hoped to live and get a job in New York City. Her occupational specialty was prison guard.

In a few days it was noticed that Alan and big dog Beaufort had disappeared from hippie hill. In about a week they were back, along with Evelyn, three dark children, and Alan's certain promise that life would be better for them in his log cabin here in Danbury. In the back seat of the car Beaufort and the kids had immediately shared dirt, bugs, food and love, and up front Evelyn had fallen for Alan as quickly as he had for her, and they have pretty much lived happily ever after.

Our old farm, my Great Aunt Elsie Nordhoff Hillsmith's place, was about 80 acres of much grown-over hilly pasture on the south end of town. Alan's log cabin, where he lived with Evelyn and Beaufort and the kids was on the north end of town, about 5 or 6 miles away. Alan used to get to his jobs around town, including our place, by driving to work on his big high-wheeled tractor. Since the pace was leisurely, Beaufort would run along with him, and, in good dog fashion, stop and say a polite hello at each farm or house they passed. The pace was such that handsome and socially adept Beaufort had time to become quite intimate with the female dogs en route, of which there were many. Since neither men nor dogs in Danbury espoused canine castration, there were a large number of puppies in town that showed evidence of Beaufort's "Blue Tick" blood in their make- up.

"Runtly" was the first of Beaufort's offspring we got to know. As a little puppy he had come to live near us at Eddie Luke Phelps' house, having been conceived and born a mile away at Stanley Phelps place where there was a thoroughbred female chow. The combination made for a strange looking dog. Friend Jim English, with uncharacteristic insensitivity, said Runtly was the ugliest dog he had ever seen. But as you will eventually see, he was a very smart dog, maybe even smarter than Jim English if you consider that his Danbury schooling was probably less complete than Jim's at Yale. While his family were both off at work, Runtly spent a lot of time at our farm.

But one day I got a phone call from Alan. "Wally," he says, "you know that little black lab bitch that lives out behind the post office. Well, Beaufort knocked her up. Her first time, and most of the puppies died. The guy who owns her brought the three living ones over here and said they are my responsibility. He's pissed. I'm trying to find out if anybody wants them. I can't keep them so I'll have to shoot them in a couple of days if nobody wants them." Sarah and I had been considering a dog but had decided to wait a while. I told Alan this and said I was sorry I could not help him.

The next day, while driving along in the car with Sarah, I innocently and foolishly let a question that was drifting around in my mind take sufficiently audible form so that Sarah heard it. "I wonder if Alan has shot those puppies yet?"

"SHOT WHAT PUPPIES YET?"

I doubt if Sigmund Freud or anyone else could ever state a more absolute rule about human nature than that one should not speak of shooting puppies in the presence of a woman who loves puppies.

In moments we had entered through Alan's massive single slab oak front door of his log cabin. On the second floor, amidst a three foot depth of children's' clothing, we found a shoe box in which were three very little puppies. It wasn't a question of "if" but just "which one?" Soon, one latched on to Sarah's thumb and started sucking. Within an hour we were back home and the puppy was sucking Sarah's finger submerged beneath the surface of a bowl of milk and gruel and thus learning how to eat and drink on his own, a technique Dale (Phelps) Cook had shown us that he regularly used to get his calves self-feeding. And the puppy had a name, "Monty."

Though he almost always handled it with aplomb in his long life, with this name we were giving our new little puppy quite a bit of baggage, some of it quite puzzling. Montfort Hillsmith, the original Monty, was Aunt Elsie's husband. He died young in 1916 so none of us ever met him. But at their farm we lived every day in the presence of his architectural and carpentry efforts to turn the 1820 farm house into a gothic cathedral. He installed a high, pointed window, exposed the beamed ceilings and hand carved a number of beautiful small details. He was an architect, but we found among his papers only a few small blueprints of gothic looking churches that had all had been stamped "rejected". He had been a Teddy Roosevelt Rough Rider, and an early member of the Boston Society of Arts and Crafts, and, with my aunt, a member of the Communist Party. He was also a little bit crazy and had no money. Several of Danbury's real old timers remembered him. One told us he rode his horse to town to get the mail in a full suit of armor. Gifford Wiggin, in his 99th year, told us that everybody knew Monty was going to die when he lost that big lawsuit. Big lawsuit? We didn't know about that. What was it about? Tell us. Gifford's answer has stuck hard in our memories ever since. He said, "Well, if nobody has told you about that, nobody in your own family or even somebody else here in town, well then, by gory, you ain't going to hear it from these lips, no sir." Unfortunately, Gifford's lips went with him when he soon turned 100 and died. We have a faint clue—at least it has to be a clue to something— in the form of an ancient undertaker's report and bill we miraculously found in a pile of scrap paper in the barn. In my Aunt's writing on the undertaker's bill are the words, "But what I want to know is was there water in her lungs when she was found in the bog?".

The last work that Alan did with me before the strong pull of logging took him forever back into the woods was to finish up my newly dug pond. We put in the overflow pipes and planted a double row of birches and poplars on the new dam, an allee, as Aunt Elsie's father, my great grandfather, had done at his Mexican ranch. I ordered from White Flower Farm my favorite white water lilies (Weller Pond) and expensive blue and yellow Japanese water iris. Using a six pack of beer as our main tool, Alan and I floundered around together in the mucky water finally planting the bulbs with our toes. The next spring I was delighted to see water lilies coming up. But the first ones to bloom were the standard New Hampshire yellow and pink and were not where I remembered planting them. Nor did the small Blue Flag iris coming in around the edges look like what I had paid so much money for. Later in the summer when eight big trout floated belly up to the surface in the too warm water, Alan admitted he had brought in the trout and a few local water lilies and iris on his own one week when we were away. So much for tough guys.

Monty, the puppy, was not much more than a month or two old when we realized that he would meet our hope in being a dog that would never need to be tied up. He never wanted to run away and he never got lost. He was soon trained to simply stay in the yard when we went away for the day. He had his own dog door into the house. On moonlit nights we would occasionally hear his door flip open in the small hours as he went out to sniff the wildlife and sometimes howl with the other dogs in the valley.

We, and Monty, were very lucky in our nearest neighbors, Lloyd and Ardell Phelps, senior members of Danbury's largest clan. Ardell and Lloyd had essentially kept my great aunt alive in her last years at the farm with no heat except fireplaces, no electricity, and no money. To keep from freezing the cold water tap ran a little bit all winter long in the kitchen's soap stone sink. Early check registers show many small drafts to several of the Phelps for firewood, chicken feed, and other items. For some time Elsie had a $500 a year income from a woman friend but this stopped and as best I can tell she eventually lived on nothing. My family does not appear to have supported her in any way until the last months of her life when they gave Ardell Phelps money to get her a new mattress, on which always proud Elsie, according to a letter from Ardell to my mother, would then not sleep. Ardell was devastated because the store would not take it back and she could not afford to buy it from my mother. Would it be OK if she let her son David use it for a while as he did not have a mattress? This was Ardell. But strong Lloyd was just as good and helpful in his gruff, huge, temperamental way. He had married Ardell, young and pregnant by another man who "had done something to her she did not understand." When we first moved in, he engaged himself as my caretaker for $40 a month by simply stating that it was so. Never one to question such authority, I agreed, but Lloyd soon got a raise and made more money helping to clear the brush and small timber from the overgrown pastures. He described life as a logger in the early days when he would ride a heavily loaded log skid down Ragged Mountain in the winter, hoping the skid would not get going too fast and overrun him and the oxen in front trying to hold it back. On the steep hill between our houses during one winter storm a car had skidded off the road. I watched as Lloyd, at 75, with a bad back and no knees, got his old logger's peavy, slipped it under the car, strained and lifted a few times and the car was skidded back into the center of the road. He had worked in the CCC during the Depression, never drank or smoked because he literally could not afford it, and never used a dirty word the entire time I knew him. Finally, one day Lloyd declared that, with all my fixing up, the farm had become an estate (accent on the first syllable) and he had gotten too old to be the caretaker anymore. He probably wanted his son Eddie Luke to take over the job, but when I chose Ronnie Moran, a friend of Alan's, he quickly said, "He's a good man. Honest. Only person in his family as far back as I can remember who's not a drunk."

As the years went on Monty, now a full grown 75 pound dog, frequently stayed with Lloyd and Ardell, which both parties loved, and made our peripatetic life possible. One time, when they were in their eighties, these true folks made, with considerable trepidation, an important request of us. Would we be sure to include in our will, "that piece of paper that you write out before you die", that Monty should go to them if Sarah and I died? We agreed.

But if Monty, on his way down the road to Lloyd's place, were to turn right at the corner and go on about 200 yards he would come to Steve Corsetti's farm. Steve was friendly and he had all kinds of animals that Monty would have enjoyed being friendly with, especially piglets running loose like puppies, but the place was guarded by an old German Shepherd who welcomed no other canines, so visiting took place on only very special occasions. Steve eventually ran a dozen or so Scot Highland cattle on our pastures. We found them so grand and picturesque that we didn't charge Steve for the pasturage, which was probably what he was counting on from the beginning. One old sow regularly came up to our place and had her piglets in the nearby woods and one cow, tellingly named Inky, quite regularly escaped the fencing and we would wake early on a summer morning and hear loud munchings in the flower garden under the bedroom window. Scot Highlanders don't take guidance well. Sometimes it would take Steve and his wife and Sarah and me all in our pajamas yelling and running around to get "Inky" and her 5 foot horn spread back into the pen.

Monty overcame his fear of Steve's dog one time on a very cold winter morning when Steve had attempted to butcher a large hog. With his throat slit the hog had escaped and spewed gallons of hot red blood around on about an acre of fresh white cold snow. Monty somehow discovered this colorful event shortly before I got there and was ravenously enjoying the dog form of children's syrup on snow. Steve was Danbury's Chief of Police, but, as he told me that morning, wiping the blood from his hands and face, he loved farming best.

Our farm, both the building itself and its historical background, in many ways stood in contrast to such surrounding primitiveness and violence as hog slaughtering. As an extreme example, we found in a back cupboard an old, heavily engraved card announcing, pretentiously, or ambitiously, "Mr. and Mrs. Montfort Hillsmith, Ragged Place, at home, 4 pm, Thursdays".

And evidence indicates that some people did come, sometimes, and from as far away as Boston. Family tradition names John Reed, the high profile young communist, among others. (But I bet they didn't come in January or February.)

One entered our building through a four inch thick front door heavily embedded with wrought iron work and displaying a small bronze satyr for a door knocker. (After Elsie died, Sarah and I removed, among other things, the door knocker. This door itself was then stolen by a Boston interior decorator and Lloyd had to make a new one as best he could.) After a small vaulted ceiling entrance hall one entered the old pine paneled living room with its tall Rumford fireplace and corbelled chimney. The main ceiling beam was 10 by 12 inch pine without a knot and barely a single grain leaving its edge for its forty foot length. The front windows were famous in the region for their hundreds of small panes and were reportedly brought from England by a friend of Monty's. Much woodwork showed signs of many hours of imaginative, artistic work by Monty himself, but the main staircase was built by a man visiting from Boston in 1913. He did not know that it was impossible to build a stair case in the small space where other early New England houses made do with ladders so he went ahead anyway and built gracefully angled steps complete with a cat viewing perch. It became my model as I took on the challenge of building a similar one to the loft in the east wing barn. My mother, who had attended a dance there when she was 13, reported that the musicians and others had at that time gained access to the loft through a secret door in an upstairs bedroom. It was wonderful to use all three fireplaces in the great central chimney, even though it was a limited wonder, especially for Sarah, to use the single closet in the entire house, small and shallow, which was located in the dining room.

The appeal of Ragged Place, the Danbury farm, probably got me when I first visited at age two in 1929, and I do remember it. Aunt Elsie had assembled her animals, dogs and cats, and probably chickens, and the Jersey cow, all in the yard to greet us after our long day's travel from Hartford. I was taken out of the car and put down in the grass to wait while the adults said their hellos. The cow decided to greet me and put her large wet grass flecked muzzle about a foot from my face. I still see it, and the view beyond over the hill and down to the bog below.

But the real pull came when I was 14 and had ridden my bike over from Maine, where I had been raking blueberries to make my fortune. Aunt Elsie had gone out early in the August morning to pick great bowls of dewy fresh sweet ripe blackberries, always a feature of the farm, for the breakfast of her only visiting relative. I had my first chance to wander alone around the house and barn. After seeing a lot, I was returning from the barn through the small shed passageway that once connected the two buildings, when I stopped to look and listen. The sun had risen rapidly and was shining through the cobweb-curtained windows. There was a humming sound, warm and friendly, perhaps of bees waking under the shingles on the south wall, and it said to me, "I, this place, am alive." On the wall hung old farm tools and a scythe on a wooden peg, also draped in cobwebs. I felt that the scythe, particularly, was patiently stilled and resting, and had been waiting for decades to be used again by someone. I had just read Frost's "North of Boston", it was 1941, still a rural prewar world, and I knew a man could be connected to almost every other man in the world, alive or dead, by swinging a scythe. My father had been teaching me. I wanted to swing this scythe, here on this farm. I wanted this farm. And so it happened that this became the first of the several places on the earth that have had a strong pull on me.

But I could not stay and become a farmer. There still was school to go to and then the Marine Corps. Then after college there was the Korean War, and then when Elsie died in in 1959 there was $3000 of back taxes to pay before anyone could get the title and we had no money. So it was only finally in 1987, in a much changed world and as a retired businessman with arthritis, that I finally bought the farm back and got to swing the scythe.

On the first night we spent there I knew that for me, at least, we had made the right move when, needing a nail, I went in search to the cellar workbench. The place had been so little used while owned by another party in the intervening years that Monty's Hillsmith's collection of nails was there, waiting for me. It was in a bronzed tin box with an embossed cover showing a romantic picture of desert camels and pyramids and the proud words "Rameses Egyptian Cigarettes". Expensive cigarettes did first came packed this way. The one photo we have of Monty shows him holding, with a certain elaborateness of hand position, such a cigarette. The box is now my nail box, better than the one I had before, and I suspect I'll keep it 'til the end.

But a more powerful, even painful experience that gave me insight into Montfort Hillsmith was discovering the true identity of the dozen or so small "Indian Burial Mounds" on the rocky hillside behind the house. I had never believed the burial mound story and I had read that during the first World War garnets and mica used in early radios had been taken from these hills. Aunt Elsie had once told me there was "Mica money" on the property. While walking the hill one day I saw an unusually straight line of raised debris and leaves running across a pit beside one of these "burial mounds". I quickly peeled back the debris and found a sturdy, long, but heavily rusted crowbar. Monty, I concluded, had been doing laborious hand mining in this ragged granite. He had finally quit here and put down the crowbar for the last time, too tired and discouraged to even carry it back to the house. I am pretty sure he never made a find or earned a dollar, but from the number of pits it is certain that he put in a lot of killing work in hope of doing so. I sat by his pit and thought about my ancestor. Compared to me, he had had no resources and struggled harder. But we both loved this crooked place, on the crooked road, and each left our own mark on it. He first, then me. Next, someone else.

Eddie Luke Phelps, Lloyd's son, and I had a particularly good time working together in the first years because his grandfather, Andrew, had done a lot of work at the place with Uncle Monty and Aunt Elsie. We were laying out the first small fenced pasture for goats and thought we had been extremely clever in our alignments for the fences between rocks and giant old maples on the hillside behind the house. Suddenly Eddie stumbled with his foot caught in a wire square of rusty old stock fencing. Just where we had planned to put up the new fence, we now found most of an old one fallen down and buried under the leaves. Eddie had some profane but loving words about his grandfather still tripping him up. That day we also found under the leaves the iron rim of a large wagon wheel. All the wood had long ago rotted away. Growing strongly in the center of the circling rim was a sturdy 18 inch diameter ash tree. What, we wondered, had happened so finally on that day when someone left this wheel lying here not to be touched again for more than 50 years?

In New Hampshire, glaciers plowing down from the north frequently dumped their loads of rocks on the south slopes of hills and mountains. Ragged Farm was on a south-facing slope, warm and pleasant, but it clearly had more than its fair share of rocks. Eddie and I walked the miles of stone walls built in the 19th century for the dual purpose of fencing in sheep and clearing the pastures. But there were many more rocks than were needed to build walls. As we walked through the pastures, now dark forests, we discovered that on every large rock, too large to move, many small rocks had been carefully piled just to get rid of them. Even knowing better, you could believe, if you wanted to, that these monuments deep in the forest were part of some ancient spiritual endeavor.

We also learned to keep an eye out for individual rocks. Most of the rocks the glacier dumped in this region were shapeless and awkward to use for walks or building purposes. The several miles of existing walls were very much what are called "farmer walls", not carefully or artistically laid, so we were always looking for rocks with a flat side, a square corner or two, and hopefully with a few nice patches of lichen growing on them. All our local young helpers at first laughed at us. Rocks for them were just something for bulldozers to push around. But eventually some helpers got the idea and would bring Sarah a rock he thought was special for her garden or me a good one for a building shape. I kept thinking that their grandfathers would have known. At Ragged Farm rocks were always part of our life. We knew some by name.

While we walked the walls, Monty and Runtly would first jump back and forth from one side to the other, convinced that the other dog had the side with more chipmunks or squirrels. Soon, however, they would each settle down on opposite sides, move along at the same pace and exhibit great cooperation in not allowing any rodent to escape from either side of the wall without at least being nipped at if not caught and eaten. Half brothers, Runtly was smarter and quicker, but Monty always had more motivation,—hunger. One day while we were all walking a newly cut ski trail up on Ragged Mountain the dogs shared a joint pinnacle of success. A very large rabbit had raced in terror into a hiding beneath a bush 10 feet in front of Sarah and me. As we stood transfixed, the dogs simultaneously leapt under the bush and emerged, Runtly with the rabbit head firmly in his mouth, Monty with his big white teeth clamping the rear quarters. Slowly, eyeing each other competitively, the dogs began to back away from each other. And continued to back away. They were strong dogs. The rabbit was not so strong. He parted in the middle. The rest took only a few moments. You have to admit that city people just don't ever get to see their dogs do things like that.

Nor would city people ever learn, as I did, that no scientific description of a dog's great smelling strength is adequate to describe what a dog can really do with his nose. After a fresh deep snowfall I went out early one cold and totally windless winter morning to walk the trail in back of our hill. Monty was with me. We were early but not earlier than several other large animals whose tracks crossed our route. As we came to a track Monty would race down it with his warm black velvety nose plowing the cold white snow, and go perhaps first to the left 25 feet and then to the right about the same distance. Even with his nose stuck down into the snowy track he would still be moving fast. He would then repeat the process, but run further down the track in each direction and would be running faster. He might have to do this a third time, but pretty quickly he would make up his mind—you could see it happen— which way the animal had run, and then he would take off after him, deer, fox, coyote, leaving me alone to study the shape of the animal's hoof or paw print so I could determine visually which way the animal had run. Monty never made a mistake. And the way he could tell—there is no other explanation—was that the faint scent left in the crystalline snow by the passing animal was fresher in the direction in which the animal had run than in the direction from which he had come. That is, fresher by perhaps two or three seconds for every 100 feet or so of the animal's track. And that's fresher by two or three seconds in a section of track that was made maybe an hour—3600 seconds— earlier. That's a good nose. Alan said only good dogs could do it, like Beaufort's offspring. It's more amazing to me than cell phones, moon rocket trajectories, or computers, all quite clearly, simply, boringly, and unarguably the products of intelligent design. But going back the millions of years in time, we can imagine and enjoyably reflect on the generations of dogs that could smell very well becoming the ones that could catch more animals, survive better, and breed more, thus reinforcing the trait over those millions of years and generations. Dogs that could not do it, if they survived at all, had to move to New York City or Florida and become gigolos. And that is proof of the benign and marvelous

nature of (God's) evolutionary workings, and of God himself if
you wish, and if you want more, you are ungrateful and won't
get it.

Sarah often favored Runtly, at least I felt so. It probably
started in our first year at the farm when Sarah had few social
contacts other than the early morning in bed visits of puppy
Runtly who came up to our house as soon as his working parents
departed for their jobs. Anyway, she was forever remarking on
how smart he was. I was reduced to insisting that if Runtly was
smart, Monty was good. But Sarah had some convincing evidence on her side. Eddie Luke had explained to us one time, and
also quite firmly to Runtly, that although he didn't mind having
a dog that visited about, he liked to have that dog at home duti-
fully waiting for his master when he got back from work. Runtly
took this to mean, among other things, that above all he should
not be seen leaving the neighborhood in our car in the late afternoon just about the time we often liked to leave for a walk in
one of the outlying attractive regions of the town. But such a
walk, with Monty and us, was the highlight of Runtly's day.
What should a dog do? He figured it out, and then, by observ-
ing him, we figured it out. As we got in the car, Runtly would
not get up on the seat in his usual place next to Monty but
would hunker on the floor until we were a mile or two away.
Then he would jump up next to Monty, give him a lick, and enjoy the rest of the trip. On the way back the process would be
reversed and he would hide down low until we let him out in
our backyard from whence he would circle back home to his
own place through the woods. "I've been out chasing the coyo-
tes off the back forty," was his response, I'm sure, to any question
from Eddie Luke. It worked, and for twelve years it enabled us to
have great, if illicit, walks with a smart dog and a good dog.

As did the dogs, I had my own several peak experiences while
at the farm, often with Monty. Grazing animals and pasture
health have always fascinated me. Homer speaks of "golden

hoofed" sheep because if managed correctly, sheep will turn a wasteland into a beautiful greensward in a short time. (Cows, you Westerners please note, will not. The pounds of cow per square inch of hoof are too great, thus cutting the turf, and their large plops kill the grass beneath rather than sprinkle fertilizer gently all around as do sheep and goats.) At Ragged Farm I had about 30 sheep and six goats in the beginning and I was attempting intense rotational grazing. Local agricultural experts had helped me to seed our pastures with the proper mix of legumes, vetch, timothy and clovers. In year three or four, when all these grasses had come on strongly, I was sitting in the middle of an healthily growing south-facing hillside pasture deeply enjoying the realization of a hard worked for and expensive dream. Monty was sitting beside me, leaning slightly on me. Even though it was a low intensity experience, I was about as happy and contented as I have ever been. Quietly, from behind us, Shandra, the bellwether goat and a daily competitor with Monty for my attention, approached. As Monty and I sat together we suddenly felt a head nudge in between us as jealous and lonely Shandra pushed in to take the place next to me. Rather than give her the customary little nip of warning, Monty moved over slightly, making room for her, while she made no effort to give him the little butt with her forehead that was her happy habit. We three sat in a row and enjoyed the rest of the evening. What more can one ask for?

Well, you can ask for Yard Island. Thirty minutes from the farm, Squam is New Hampshire's prettiest lake and Yard Island the lake's prettiest place. The island is made up of several little islets all covered with small evergreens and berry bushes. They sit on pure, hard, white granite sand with crystal clear water lapping their beaches and shorelines. The view straight down the lake's main reach is of Mount Chocorua. I had long held the dream of spending the night on Yard and the time had come. Approaching in our little old boat one late August evening, I

gave Monty some lengthy and soothing instructions—you have
to try— on how he must obey me absolutely because it was a
private island and I did not want the patrolling ranger in his
boat to either see or hear us. We arrived about an hour before
sunset. We pulled the boat up to the south side of a little white
sandbar separating two islets and both got out into six inches of
water. Across the sandbar and in the little north bay we both at
once saw three loons paddling slowly in a circle. I held Monty
for a minute or so, urging him not to bark at or to chase these
birds. I released him slowly and he gradually waded in up to dog
paddling depth and joined the birds in their stately and unper-
turbed circling of the little bay. The dog's black head with white
tipped muzzle looked just like another loon. As they continued
to circle, the voice of neither bird nor dog broke the silence of
the early evening.

Later, when the ranger, making his rounds, came and circled
the island to check, I had pulled the boat up as far as I could and
covered the stern and motor with an old green blanket. Monty
and I crouched in the brush and glowered at him. He never saw
us. At dusk some bourbon for me and a large lamb chop for each
of us was supper. We slept on the smallest islet, about 50 feet
wide. Monty, sleeping three feet from my ear, woke me in the
middle of the night with deep, very serious growls. Trying to go
back to sleep, I wondered what possible living creature large
enough to threaten us could also be on this tiny dot of land.
When I woke in the morning Monty was gone, but in a half
hour or so he came walking slowly back across the sandbar from
the other islets where he had been exploring and sniffing to his
heart's content. He was a good dog.

When Alan had needed help lifting the biggest rocks back
onto the walls from which they had fallen sometime in the past
hundred years or so he had brought along a friend for help.
Ronnie Moran could pick up a rock almost as big as himself,
admittedly a small self, but still a feat. Once he had started work-

ing regularly for us our friendship grew quickly, became one of the best I have ever had, and lasted for ten years until we sold the farm and moved beyond the small geographic circle in which Ronnie had decided he would enjoy his life. Not only did he help me, but eventually he became willing to work directly and knowledgeably for Sarah in the flower gardens. Men did not do this in Danbury. Vegetable gardens yes, flower gardens no. But Ronnie was different. He was willing to learn, was naturally bright, had some aspirations, and he loved to talk. Joking and sparring was daily fare.

"Ronnie, you're late. It's almost nine. You know I won't tolerate that. What happened?" I asked with the sternest false anger I could summon up.

"Oh, I stopped in to see my grandmother on the way over."

"But you called me last night and said you'd be here at eight." Ronnie always called and was never late.

" Well, you know, things here in New Hampshire aren't quite like what you're used to down in those cities. You got elevators and traffic lights and everything to keep you moving on schedule, and you got policemen with pistols to help you if you run into any trouble."

"Sounds like you ran into some trouble this morning?"

"A little, but it was just a personal matter with my grandmother. An unexpected visitor."

I had to go along. "Oh, I'm sorry. I hope she's OK."

"She's OK, but I'm not sure the other party is."

"All right, all right Ronnie, for Christ sake, tell me, what the hell happened."

"Well, I'm sure its not as bad as what happens down in the cities in the morning, probably every morning, what with crime and all that stuff you have there, but when I got to my grandmother's place this morning she was standing on the porch with a broom in her hands waiting for me to help her chase the bear out of her kitchen and yelling at me for being late."

After he had told the story, in detail, the best I could manage in comment was that it must have been a very large bear to delay Ronnie for half an hour. In the future I would allow 15 minutes for standard bear chasing jobs.

Grandma, he told me over time, had been the central person in his childhood. Her little old ramshackle house on North Road had been, in a sea of family alcohol, a safe island for him and many of the kids. They often lived there. And despite the poverty, he had many happy childhood memories of life at Grandma's. He particularly liked to tell me about playing childhood games on summer evenings with his siblings and cousins. Tag, kick the can, sardines. The best was Hide-and-Seek where you tried to run from a hiding place in the darkening woods surrounding the house all the way to the big, round, flat rock by the front door. If you could get there before the kid who was "It" saw you, then you yelled "Allie-Allie-in-Free" and every body else could run back from their hiding places and got in safe, just as they were safe at the house itself. They called the big rock the Allie-Allie-in-Free rock.

Sadly enough, Grandma's sober example was not enough to keep Ronnie as a teenager from following the drinking life of the rest of his family. He told me that in a high school class each kid had been asked to describe their goals for life. He had stated his as getting an easy job that would give him just enough money to stay drunk all the time. With a well developed sense of irony he told me that, although his classmates thought this was going to be a difficult goal, he had accomplished it quickly and permanently. He was drunk for fifteen years and would surely have gone down in the ongoing shipwreck of his family and friends if he had not luckily been thrown one small life preserver. A chance visit from a sober uncle took him to a single AA meeting which showed him, for the first time, in his mid-thirties, that there was another way. He believed, and rescued himself. When we became friends he had not had a drink for ten years. For

Christmas he gave me, as men do, a bottle of liquor. I thought hard and gave him a picture book of historical trucks. He owned five, real ones, all old if not historical. I think it may have been the first book anyone had ever given him.

Once or twice a year I'd get my own old pickup, call Monty, Runtly, and Ronnie, and we would pick up the beer cans along the several wooded miles of Wiggin Road. We all enjoyed this cleanup activity, although the dogs never quite figured out exactly what they were supposed to be doing. Ronnie and I believed that between the two of us we could figure out who had thrown out each beer can we found based on our knowledge of what brand the local men each drank. "Well, here's another Billy Cook," Ronnie would say as he picked up a Coors can and threw it in the truck." I would add, "This one looks like a Clem Smith to me," as I threw in a Budweiser. One time when the game had gotten a little old and I was trying to pick up some broken glass from a green beer bottle I said to Ronnie, "I wonder how much longer New Hampshire will be the only New England state that doesn't have a bottle deposit law?"

Ronnie said, "Well, you don't believe in them do you? They don't do any good."

"Of course they do," I replied. "I'll bet there aren't half as many beer bottles and cans alongside the roads in Maine or Vermont as in New Hampshire."

"We've got too many laws already," Ronnie, a true son of New Hampshire, admonished me. "You know, there wouldn't be half this many cans if they hadn't passed that other law about it a few years ago."

I felt he must be crazy and didn't know what he was talking about, but I had forgotten that Ronnie knew a lot more about drinking than I did. He was right, if in a limited way.

"The reason," he said, with clear satisfaction of knowing something I didn't, "is that they passed a law here a while ago that it was a crime to have an open liquor or beer container in your car. So everybody tosses them out the window the minute they're finished. Don't want to be caught with one in the car. If they see a cop coming, they throw them even before they're finished. Makes for a lot of trash along the road."

So much for the bottle bill.

Ronnie had a keen interest in economic theory and trapped me into believing that I could help him into new and better understandings. Flattering though his belief was, I am not sure it was justified. I lost our first debate. The subject was argued for several seasons but I finally agreed with him that paving more of Danbury's 90 miles of dirt roads would be a mistake. It would take wealth out of the town because you had to borrow money to do it and pay interest to those big bankers down in Concord, and you had to buy macadam from an oil company and some of that money probably ended up as far away as Saudi Arabia. It was better if the selectmen would just keep using our own tax money right here in town by buying gravel from one of the Phelps gravel pits and by paying our own freely elected road agent, Ronnie's brother, to grade the roads once or twice a year. I knew enough not to argue that there were any offsetting benefits in being able to drive faster and more enjoyably over roads without any bumps, even if I had still believed it, which, after some years in Danbury, I had begun to doubt anyway.

I also learned that the classic economic rule about adjusting price to make supply and demand equal is not an entirely sufficient guide for a good business. I was often unhappy that I couldn't get Ronnie to work with me in the spring and the fall because so many other people were after him as well. And he himself at these times would seem to be unhappy about being so busy that he didn't have time to eat or sleep. He said he found it too hard to say "No" to people and was always promising more than he could do. I explained to him that if he had gone to the Harvard Business School they would have instructed him to gradually raise his prices until the demand shrank to just the amount that would keep him busy and he would never have to say "No" to anybody again, and he would be richer.

"Well, I don't think that would work too well, really", he said. "Yesterday I did Haddie Huntoon's little parsnip patch for her, rototilled it. It's only about two passes with the tractor. Takes more time to load and unload than it does for the job. But she's been doing parsnips there all her life. I started charging them $25 when Orville was still alive. What would she think if I told her it was $35 now that he's dead? And I think she's the only one left in the whole town who still does parsnips, anyway."

"Yeah, you're right there", I said, agreeing with him. Haddie had once proudly given me one of her freshly dug parsnips in March.

"And I already do charge some people a lot more for things, like your friend Karen over in Andover. I give the chicken manure away to some people just to get rid of it, but I charge her $50 a truck load. She'd pay $100 if I asked her, but I'd still be driving all the way over to Andover."

I eventually began to see Ronnie as a private sector distributor of economic equity and I stopped arguing with him. It was only with agony and apologies that he raised the prices he charged me once in ten years, but Dick Chase, newly arrived from Connecticut, got hit pretty hard. Ronnie knew I would find out, and I think he was trying to show me he had learned something. But Dick will get his money's worth in friendship and conversation and can also consider some of his payment to be a contribution to a United Fund which does not otherwise exist in Danbury.

On January 18 of 1998 in Northern New England and Canada nature went slightly, just ever so slightly, off course and changed everything. If the temperature had been two degrees warmer, 33 instead of 31, the several inches of rain that was falling would not have ended up as tons and tons of ice on every tree and bush and every phone and power line. The toppling of the giant steel "hydro" towers in Canada, lying on their bent and broken sides like slain giants of old, at first seemed to me to be the most impressive damage done, and probably it was for the whole region. But it was as we slowly began the cleanup of the damage done to our own place, Ragged Farm, that an important change in Sarah's and my hearts began.

Ron Moran with his tractors, trucks, chain saws, splitters and chippers came to help us, as did good friend and neighbor strong Ivan Ourusoff. Alan Brownell came. I will not forget him sawing up our largest white birch under which I had just completed a Japanese wooden gate through a stone wall. These men do not use dull saws. The great white trunk, perhaps 100 years old, became 18 inch billets ready for the firewood splitter in minutes. A group of six smaller white birches with Sarah's euonymus at their base were flat down. We would never again see them in the fall with the bright red standing out against the white bark. My helpers knew what was happening perhaps as well as I did. They wanted to save birches by pulling them back up straight again and tying them with ropes. We were told they would not survive, but these guys did it anyway. Sixty-five foot tall trees raised up from flat and braced with ropes!

The remaining rows of 180 year-old maples which had been planted when the farm was first built were already very close to the end of their lives, and many now had lost their few remaining good limbs. The most venerable one, over the goat shed in the back yard, was left with one live limb. We let it stand but probably shouldn't have. The big oaks were the most difficult, and most expensive, to handle. Big branches had broken off high in their canopies and not fallen down. We finally had to hire a man to come in with a boom truck to reach the dangerous limbs and bring them down. But the symmetry of the great branching canopies was gone for good.

This work was discouraging. At this date, our major projects to bring the farm back to its original splendor had all been accomplished and we were getting used to doing a certain amount of maintenance work rather than enjoying always just the fun of creating. But this storm was not even maintenance. This was cleaning up destruction. We began to get up in the morning without our usual enthusiasm. And finally, but irrevocably, the thought entered our minds, for both of us about the same time, that maybe we had done enough, maybe we needed something new and easier.

We looked back at what we had done in our 13 years, how much we had enjoyed the creative aspects of the work, and what a nice place we would be leaving for the next inhabitants to enjoy, and these reflections made us feel good. Here's what we listed out as our efforts and their accomplishments:

It had started with Eddie Luke, an expert with concrete, putting in new basements under the barn and house. Either you start there or you are going to be in trouble eventually. Likewise roofs, with insulation. Outside, five pastures were cleared, reseeded, fenced and gated, with the gates carefully made following plans we brought back from a walking trip in Cornwall. My father had always told me Ragged Place had no water on it and was too dry to live on, but Alan and I found and developed three new surface springs using special divining equipment from Budweiser. These were small springs so the Scot Highlanders with their great horns could drink only one at a time. It was fun to watch them push around on a hot day struggling for their turn to get one of those powerful two or three gallon sucking slurps. We also dug, and nature filled, the quarter acre fenced-in pond. Ardell Phelps, myself, male grandchildren and the dogs were about the only mammals that swam there, but the sheep, goats, horse and cattle wanted to and were always testing the fence.

Sarah discovered early on that every time Lloyd cut down a tree and she cleared the brush and weeds from a patch on the hill behind the house that lupin, yellow lilies and narcissus sprang up almost immediately. They had been waiting in Aunt Elsie's old garden beds for more than 50 years and needed only the sun to wake them up. Eventually Sarah had nine perennial beds with everything from asters to zinnias as well as long borders of day lilies, foxgloves, daffodils, and islands of phlox. Wherever we traveled we took buckets of freshly cut flowers.

A special project of Sarah's was to develop our picnic site up by the old gravestone granite ledge under which "Montfort Hillsmith & his Wife Elsie" and "Five Faithful Friends", their horses and dogs, were buried. From a strong, long limb of the old oak tree that sheltered the grave site we hung the best single rope swing any kids had ever seen. As their great, great, grand nephews stood on their gravestone starting their long, arching and circling swing, Monty and Elsie beneath were surely happy. We searched for and found three very large rocks so well shaped that they alone made up a fireplace. Ronnie moved up the old outhouse from behind the barn. As we sat by the fire and drank and ate and played, we could look down to the wild Danbury Bog and up to Ragged Mountain Ski Area, each just a mile away.

We cut and used our own cross country ski trails on our back 50 acres. We built a fountain in the garden so that when you sat on the new terrace you could hear and see water. Having always loved the classic design of the Adirondack log lean-to, I got Alan to help me build a big one for an animal shelter on the main hill pasture. But it took a really skilled carpenter, Harold Jones from Hill, to help me finish a garden Gazebo the design of which we took from the famous ones at Mohonk House. The look of a lacy tapestry of branches supporting a pine slab roof is not easy to achieve, especially using Hornbeam, also called Ironwood. But it did end up having exactly the appearance of something Montfort Hillsmith would have designed and built and this made us feel good.

Not the least, we had redesigned and rebuilt all the back rooms of the house itself, including the second floor, and the east wing. A new kitchen at the sunny end, two baths moved and two new ones and a bedroom added. There were no plumbers available except an old man with no car that Sarah daily drove in from Bristol until brother Frank and wife Gerry saved the day and came up from Sudbury. Microwave electronic engineers make excellent plumbers. There were no licensing requirements, no building codes, and no inspectors in Danbury.

We built a sun deck suspended between the house and the barn which became a favorite eating and drinking spot and, despite Lloyd's warnings that it weakened and spoiled cars, we added a two car heated garage and a paved driveway. Page and Taylor re-laid the brick hearth for the big living room fireplace. Our painter for ten years, Jim Laro, was inexpensive, speedy and never spilled a drop—and never used a drop cloth--and was colorblind. Sarah selected every color for every room by herself, and before she was through knew practically every Benjamin Moore shade by name and number.

It was a lot of fun and we were lucky to be able to do it.

We had lots of great parties there, summer and winter, and our first batch of grandchildren got to know us there. It was a great place for dogs and we made good friends with a handful of strong men.

When the day finally came to go, the satisfaction that we felt about the good life we had had at Ragged Place and our sureness that, nonetheless, it was time to move on was, of course, tinged with some sadness about what we were leaving behind. But, as it turned out, we were not going to carry away just memories.

Ronnie had helped us move, and in his several trips he had sized up our brand new modern condominium in Grantham. Several weeks after the move-in he arrived again at our door in one of his trucks. After a few words of greeting he said, "Well, I have noticed that in this fancy place everything is sort of city-like and you don't have anything in the way of good rocks. I'm pretty sure you'll be wanting some so I brought you one. After my grandmother died this spring I decided it was better to tear down her little old house than try to fix it up. I graded the place off flat. But I saved this for you," he said, walking toward the back of the truck. Reaching it, he put his hand up on the tailgate next to a large, round, flat rock and said, "It's the Allie-Allie In Free Rock."

As time went by we knew that such a repository and touchstone of memories could not be left behind when we moved from Grantham to Truro. So now it sits in our garden here at the tip of Cape Cod and reminds us of the strong and sentimental men and the smart and the good dogs we knew in our years at The Danbury Farm. Thank you, Ronnie.

# THE WAY IT HAPPENED

We were fishing together in the headwaters gorge of New Zealand's Waikaia River when the symptoms of the disease that finally killed Harry Watson first arrived and disrupted his athletic grace and balance. We were both frightened, but it was only a brief experience and we seemed quickly to forget it.

In the gorge, the sandstone rock walls at the bottom are carved to the smooth curving shapes that water likes. Above, the banks are steep and grass covered, reflecting their green color onto the slowly moving water below. The morning sunlight was making its way into the mouth of the gorge, flickering through the overhanging branches of large old beech trees and illuminating brightly the surface of only some of the water, leaving the back eddies in dark shadow.

I had climbed high up on a wall to get a good photograph of the gorge and of Harry moving into it. Fishing would not be easy because the water between the vertical walls got deep very quickly and there would be no place to stand. Looking down, I guessed a depth of ten feet. But I also saw what Harry was heading for. A short distance into the gorge before it got too deep there was a large rock with its flat top just beneath the water's surface. He would wade to the rock, clamber up and be in a perfect spot for me to take a picture of him casting dry flies upstream. The backlighting of the sun would show off the long, flat loops of his expertly cast line. As I watched, he waded and climbed. Once securely on the rock he tried to stand up but could not. He lost his balance and fell into the swirling green liquid of the stream. Cursing, he repeated the maneuvers, and fell in again. On the rock the third time, dripping wet and breathing hard, he remained on his hands and knees and cried out, partly to himself and partly to me, "Something's wrong. The light on the water. I can't keep my balance."

I yelled back to him words I still now painfully hear and even then knew were wrong. "Harry, you just had too much to drink last night."

We moved, more easily, back downstream and finished the day fishing from the comfortable gravel bars of the pastoral, clear and gentle, grass banked lower Waikaia, so friendly and inviting, so full of happy sheep, that no dark thoughts survive there.

Later, back home in Barnstable, Harry continued the life of a divorced bachelor. Though he had been a Marine, a teacher, and college admissions dean, his real life was artistic creation. He carved and painted wooden fish and painted pictures. He sold them, and he never stopped working. He had several women friends, some he played cards with, some he made love to. He pursued large striped bass in Cape Cod Bay with a fly rod and 8 pound test line and he was with us annually for salmon fishing on the Miramachi in New Brunswick. But he seemed to get weaker and old rapidly. There were moments of embarrassment and indignity when balance, coordination or strength failed him. There were probably many of them, but my wife Sarah and I witnessed one of them.

He was being host to a small group of us at a cook out on Barnstable's Sandy Neck and he had a young grandson helping him with the fire and grilling of hamburgers. Though all of us had had a cocktail or two, Harry, whose habits I knew, had been careful to stay in control of himself. I believe he had particular hopes to show us and his grandson that he was still strong and capable. When the full moon suddenly broke out from behind a bank of clouds we all turned to look up at it. In doing this, Harry fell over backward next to the grill and the grandson. He lay there, writhing slowly, physically disoriented and emotionally devastated. I could see his face. I felt so sorry for him that on impulse I threw myself down next to him to imply that anyone could do this; it was just a normal funny thing to do.

But of course it wasn't. It was Parkinson's disease. By the time he got the diagnosis, or by the time he told me, he had been struggling with balance and motor control so noticeably that it wasn't a thunderclap of bad news. On his last trips to the Miramichi he hadn't attempted to wade the river for fishing, but instead just sat on the bank and talked with our old guide.

The last year of his life was painful and cruel to both Harry and his friends and family. He became essentially bedridden and for distraction was forced to watch hours of gruesome, blaring television. If a friend came to visit it did not help much because speech was too difficult for him and he was very deaf. His mind was still going and he wanted to express himself, but he couldn't. If it happened that he had just taken some of his powerful medicine, he was much better and would get up and could speak for a while. But on those occasions he would perversely, if understandably, try to prove that he was OK and didn't need help. It was a hard game to play.

On my very last visit to him I noticed he had cleared away all the pictures and other things that accumulate around a sick person's bed and had in front of him a solitary picture of a strong and good-looking World War I Army officer in uniform at the front in France. Harry had told me about his father. His first story, told to me 40 years ago eating lunch on the sunny banks of the Matane River in Quebec, was that he had died quite young in an accident when his car hit a tree. Some years later after we had become good friends and we were alone one night in the little Miramichi log cabin, he told me that his father had been a secret binge alcoholic and was drunk when he hit the tree. On one of our last trips to New Zealand, around the campfire late in the evening when we were just beginning to see and talk about the ends of our own lives, he told me that he had finally come to the conclusion that his father, with a troubled life, had purposefully killed himself by hitting the tree.

I tried to offer a conversation about the picture and his father but the only intelligible words he could raspingly breathe out were, "My father." I sat with him, but it didn't seem to help. He was in pain and agony. Taking a chance, I put my hand on his bald head and he sighed and nodded slightly. He may have been asleep, and dreaming of his father, a few minutes later when I left. I wish he could have died right then.

About a month later I got the phone call from Harry's nearby close friend John. Harry was dead. At 2 AM he had gotten up and tried to go down the cellar stairs to his workshop. The stairs were steep, had primitive handrails and were never well lit. Waiting at the bottom was a cold, hard, concrete floor. He fell, he hit his head, and was soon dead. But, despite this report, despite what John had been told, for me this was not the way Harry died, not the way it happened. I knew another story.

The Ahuriri River valley, about 100 miles north of the Waikaia, is not pastoral. It is a mountain valley with snow clad Mount Cook, New Zealand's tallest, sometimes visible at the northern end when it is not storming. The river wanders in a broad gravely bed down the middle of the half-mile wide valley floor. Clouds from the Tasman sea roll in over the valley's western rock ridged ramparts, and on the other side smaller slabs of rock break upward very sharply, seeming to pierce the skin of the earth, and leave short steep talus slopes. The little used, single track, dirt road is sometimes visible miles ahead as it crests over an undulation in the valley floor on its way to disappearing in the headwater's forest. Trees are few and the grass is so poor that no cattle or sheep are any longer grazed here although old rusted fence lines give evidence that at one time they were. There are no buildings of any sort. It is deserted and lonely.

And that is why, I guess, that Harry and I like it so much. Winter has returned to New England and we are now here again on our last trip to New Zealand together. As we do occasionally, Harry and I have separated from Syd, Carl, Chas, and John and head upriver for a day or two while they fish the bigger water below. Harry is an even more avid headwaters fisherman than I. Sometimes, when he was still going strong, he would spend most of his day walking miles upstream searching for good fish in shallower water and then have only an hour or two of actual fishing before walking back down the river banks in the late New Zealand dusk. We have also shared for a long time, in contrast to the others who call us just lazy, a strong preference for camping, as we did when we were boys, with the least equipment possible, emulating frontiersmen or Indian Scouts or maybe even the unencumbered animals that just lie down and sleep where they are when night comes. We have fishing tackle, our locally purchased $15 sleeping bags, a dirty frying pan, tin cups, a couple of cans of beans and hash and a jar of instant coffee. No rain gear or extra clothes, no ax for firewood, no flashlight, no folding table or tent. There is a piece of canvas we found beside the road, in case it rains, and a bottle of bourbon, in case we need it. These latter are the only nonessentials that separate us from our youth or from the animals that live and die here in this valley.

In late afternoon we stop the car for our first camp at a rise in the road which gives a broad view ahead. The river at this point is across the valley but will be a pleasant walk to start fishing in the morning. We drink and eat and then sit beside our campfire of broken sticks and brush for a long time. There are stars, the big valley is silent except for an occasional real or imagined animal cry, and we are very happy.

The morning brings need to prepare tackle for the day. Under Harry's tutelage for many years, I am competent. A blood knot for a new tippet I can do, but I use my leaders longer than I should because a needle knot for a new one is almost beyond my eyes and finger control. I love to watch Harry do it. His glasses have old bacon grease and lint on them. With smoke and ashes from the breakfast fire blowing across our laps, with Harry's coffee cup precariously perched on a rock keeping warm by the fire just a few inches from his elbow, a cigarette dangling first from his mouth and then put down in the middle of the looping nylon leader material waiting to be tied onto his line, Harry's fingers are a calm center of precise movement as he skillfully and deliberately ties a perfect knot amidst this total mess of disorganization. There is certainly no trembling sign, or Parkinson's lack of muscle control, when he is concentrating his skill on his lifelong passion.

He announces that he is going upstream today. Since we separate and fish alone during the day, I point down river to a big meander and say I'll start there. We hear thunder several miles up in the head of the valley, unusual so early. It doesn't mean it's going to rain down here and spoil our day, but if it rains much up there, the water level in the river will, soon after, rise rapidly because there is little spongy material in these gravel laden mountain valleys. We have all had quite a bit of wet experience with rising water. Harry's is the worst. His most colorful evening fireside tales are of life threatening dramas about being caught on the wrong side of the river needing to cross over to get home. What we do know is that he is unwilling to take the time, as we do, to find a strong straight sapling to cut down and make into a secure wading pole. He revels, and we have seen him do it, in just grabbing for use the nearest big cumbersome rotten log or a curving branch of a hemlock tree with so many twigs and needles on it that it has even more water resistance than does his body. He falls, all his gear gets wet, he swims, he loses his hat, but he makes it. Perversely, and proudly.

I am anticipating this, and while he is having his third cup of coffee and his third cigarette—behavior which he rationalizes under his doctrine of "compensatory immoderation", just as a pint of ice cream and a pint of bourbon taken in quick succession offset each other—I cut two good saplings from a grove behind us and then casually offer him one. But I don't get away with it. He huffs and states that he is not going to carry that thing around all day. My feelings are hurt, but I don't want to tell him that I think he may really need to be more careful now. His strength and balance are significantly weaker. I figure if I quickly leave first, he might, in my absence, pick it up.

"OK, but it's yours if you want it," I say, and then pick up my stuff and prepare to leave. "I'll see you when I see you," I add.

"OK. I going way up, probably. See you later."

Neither of us carry a watch in New Zealand, preferring to let the sun, our stomachs, our bodies, our pleasure, tell us what to do and when. It is a wonderful feeling.

Downstream, where I am heading, I see the sun flashing on the big meanders. The anticipation of a day's fishing begins to fill me, but I walk slowly over the gentle terrain, enjoying the sparse flowers and the tracks of small animals on the dusty earth. About halfway is a knoll providing a little village for a dozen rabbits, each now warming their ears and tan bodies in the morning sun outside their burrow holes. They stay long enough to greet me, but then hop inside just to be safe.

Starting at the lower end of the meanders, I have not fished long when I decide casting would be better from the opposite bank. I move up around a corner where I think the wading across will be easier, but I am suddenly surprised, very surprised, to discover that I am not alone here after all. On a small gravel bar jutting into the water on the opposite side, as if having come here for a river bank drink, but immobile and silent, eyes strongly fixed on me, stands a large, black, old bull. He is not threatening, but, as bulls are, a little intimidating. Partly, it is the surprise of his being here at all.

I feel friendly, and think he does also, but I don't feel it's necessary to cross the river just at his gravel bar. I move on upward intending to cross above where I will not have to face him head on. He must have been left here during a final roundup of cattle. Maybe too wild to catch, maybe too old to bother with. How long has he been alone here?

I look back once and see that he has turned his head so that his eyes can follow me as I move upstream, but he has not moved his body position. I turn away again and move forward, but as I do so he utters a loud bellow. I am puzzled. He wasn't bellowing before. Why has he started? But I keep moving on upstream. Then he gives two more sequences of descending strength and volume. As I walk further, deserting him, he continues to give sporadic bellows, usually three in descending power. Finally, I am out of range of his cries and return to a concentration on fishing.

I catch two trout, but it has been hard work. After lunch on a sand bar softer than most, I lie down and fall asleep while watching sunlit bubbles moving by on a calmer bit of water. I awake in the same position, see the same bubbles, and fall into a lazy speculation questioning how might I know whether I have been asleep for ten minutes or ten years, and does it make any difference anyway?

Late in the afternoon I am still fishing in the fast waters above the meanders. Turning to head back down I soon realize that the water has been rising, but I am comfortably on the home side. I approach the meanders and the corner where the bull was in the morning. I have not heard him during the day and do not expect to see him, but I do now hear a much feebler three notes of moaning, and he is there after all. He is lying down in just the same spot on the bar where he stood earlier, but the water has risen and now surrounds the fore part of his body. I notice that the gravel to his rear has been strangely scoured in a deep and prominent arc. I see that it is caused by the repeated motion of a hind leg that, as I watch, starts pushing and rocking the body forward and back over the fulcrum of his folded short front legs. For a few moments he is still, and then again he starts to moan the same three low notes while the rear leg pushes against the gravel. He is trying to get up. But he cannot do it. I watch. Again, he is very still and silent for several minutes. When next he starts to moan, it is almost a bellow and the leg and hoof push and gouge deeply in the gravel. I watch, and finally I know. This giant creature, this old black bull, is going to lie here on the gravel bar, the last place he has come to, and where he has lain down sometime during the day after I had left, unable to get up, and he will struggle and bellow, and then slowly he is going to die. Tonight? Tomorrow? Next week?

He is so large that it makes the thought of his dying hard to believe or understand. I have not seen many large animals dead of natural causes, much less seen them dying. I found an old dead seagull once—they live to be 65—feathers smoothly arranged and nested comfortably in the grass high on the seaward crest of our big dune overlooking the beach where he had spent his life catching bait fish and stealing bites of sandwich from generations of delighted children. Then another time, when the aged German Shepherd of my New Hampshire neighbor wandered off one night into the first snowstorm of the winter and didn't come back, we found him the next morning, not too far from home, curled up comfortably, snow on his ears, under the low protecting boughs of a hemlock tree sound asleep, forever. But the bull, because he is still alive, is so large, and is struggling so, pulls me in. As I watch, I would like to go over and comfort him. Put my hand on his head. I think about it. This might comfort me, but not him, I realize, and there is no way I could cross the river in the now high, fast water. I hope Harry is not trying to cross.

I watch a few moments longer and then turn and head for home, looking forward to telling Harry about the bull. Even though it is fairly late, I arrive back before him. I'm thinking about having a cup of tea when I notice the wading stick that I cut for him lies where I left it leaning against the front bumper of the car. As the first shot of worry goes through me I decide it's late enough to skip tea and have a drink. I gather wood and light a fire. It will be a welcoming beacon as it gets darker. He will be able to see the fire and come walking diagonally across the valley floor, and I will see him coming. But he doesn't come. So I sit with my drink where I can watch for the first hoped for glimpse of him coming down. He's a crazy guy, worse than crazy, but I love him.

Eventually, I get hungry and open our two cans of beans. I am careful to leave the tops held on by enough metal so that they can be bent back and used as handles, hobo style. Placing them by the fire to warm I have one more small pour of bourbon. He doesn't come.

I eat. I have a tea and decide to head for the river. If he has fallen over trying to cross upstream somewhere and has been unable to get to shore in the fast water, he will float down until he comes to the meanders. He'll be able to get out on a bank there, and, hopefully, on our side.

It's pretty dusky—it will be dark coming back—but I know my way. I am surprised to find the rabbits are still up when I come to their knoll. They are less frightened than ever, but I pass by as quickly as I can without stepping in a burrow.

I arrive at the river bank below the bull's gravel bar, and I start searching as I work upstream. The water is very high and has been depositing debris on the far bank. I don't hear any sounds from the bull, but fairly soon I see him. Or, what I see is a mound of material in the spot where he was before, with the river now swishing around the entire hulk and over all but the highest part. Soon I see that it is his head and shoulders, only, that are above the water. I see what looks like a branch sticking up from his head, but his head has been turned sideways and it is one horn now thrusting upward that I see. It doesn't look as if he is, or even could be, still breathing.

I move up until I am directly across from him, studying him so intently that at first I do not see that the strong river current flowing over him has lodged another body up against his side. However, it is a body, and though it's too dark to tell for sure, as soon as I turn my eyes to it, I see Harry. Now on the riverbank together with the old bull is my friend Harry Watson, and this, this is the way, on the Ahuriri River in New Zealand, that it happened.

# OFF AND RUNNING WITH LARRY KOHLBERG, 1945

**********

"Every psychology textbook published in the last quarter-century touches upon Kohlberg's work." Harvard Graduate School of Education News, October 1, 2000

**********

In 1917 the Russian proletariat found their strength, rose up, and threw off the yoke of the Czars. It took the spirit of revolt 28 years—no E-mail—to reach Andover, Massachusetts in 1945. When it arrived one March night, a small group of boys at Phillips Academy worked secretly through the school's darkened dormitories with argument and exhortation and secured enough pledged votes to elect on the following day the senior class president from the ranks of the non-fraternity students for the first time in the school's long history. This vote overthrew a power structure as fully established as that of the Czars. One teacher, of international scholarly repute, was heard to say it was the greatest revolt since the battles of Lexington and Concord. His field was romantic poetry.

While, certainly, in our small rebel group there were young idealists—Larry Kohlberg, then my best friend, would be the prime example—and we had as our secret faculty advisor a prominent liberal American History teacher who subsequently became Dean of Students at Harvard, none the less my own memory of the event does not have it richly infused with high purpose, noble causes or historic climaxes. Neither did we feel any particular strong enmity toward the fraternity boys. They were good guys, just a little more athletic and social than we were. Two were in our group. We did it, at least in my memory, because it was a challenge, because we thought we could, and it would be exciting and interesting to see what happened the next day.

I can't remember what happened the next day, which is unfortunate, a problem in writing memoirs. But I do know that the election held and was not challenged. Len Richardson, our candidate, became class president. His career has been in teaching and he rose to private school headmaster in California. Brot Bishop, the fraternity boy who would have won, became President of the very successful Pendleton Woolen Mills (a family concern) in Oregon and has been an extremely valuable Trustee and supporter of PA for many years. A good guy.

But it is possible that we were ahead of the wave and leaders of change, whether we knew it or not. PA usually is. Our revolt was followed in a few years by the abolition of fraternities at PA and other prep schools in New England. And I do remember enjoying for a while a slightly heady sense of personal power. The ability to manipulate one's social or political environment was new and exciting, but ultimately for me, at that time, not as much fun as working and playing in the physical world. ( My favorite and best courses at PA were Geometry, up to but not including spherical trigonometry, and Physics up to, but not including the formula for the precession of a gyroscope. Now you know some very precise things about me!)

So, along with the vote for class president, a political success on which I did not build for the future, there were two other events that started off the first year of my free life and which have had, along with Larry Kohlberg, a strong influence on my development.

The first was an address given that year to the entire school by an awesome visitor. PA boys and young men were so important to winning the victory against the Germans and the Japanese—I studied the war map every day on the front page of the Boston paper—that none other than Henry L. Stimson, then Secretary of War, came from Washington, or perhaps the battlefield itself, to Andover to speak to us. Just his old fashioned, honest, title was outstanding, and he told us how our PA predecessors had already made an heroic and critical difference (George Bush senior, among others), and how the nation's hopes for victory hung on the sense of duty and patriotism of boys like us. While I became a little fearful of just what it was I might be required to do and how soon, he quickly captured and enlisted me. Though I have never become a flag waver, and make a point of distancing myself from their cheap valor, nonetheless, since youth I have always had a deep and comfortable sense that I was one of the group—a quite imperfect and unimportant one, but nonetheless one—of the group of people that were proprietors of this nation, and that in turn it would be my duty to make any sacrifice necessary for it. I have been happily free of any of the frustrating sense of alienation now so understandably common with younger people and even with some of my peers. I probably got some of this ethic from my father (Kipling was his favorite author, after Darwin), my P.A. teachers, and that stretcher-bearing pacifist of the bloody front lines in Italy, Jimmy Goodwin. But I believe it was Stimson that closed the sale, and I thank him for it. When I discovered 5 years ago that the great man had not left either Washington or the battlefield just to address us, this very select group, but had come to Andover to Chair the School's Trustee meeting and probably only incidentally spoke to us, I was amused and pleased with my boyhood naivety but still hold to my convictions as strongly as ever. (Patriotism, if that's what it is, is easier for one past combatant age, but harder under the courant leadership of another Phillips Academy Bush!)

March 2, 1945, was my 18th birthday and my memory has me going alone to the Marine Corps recruiting station in the old Post Office in downtown Hartford, signing papers, and raising my right hand and swearing in. The Sergeant's name was Harris—(yes, I remember his name)— and was so good at his job that though I was scared, I felt I had joined a warmly welcoming and invincibly strong group of boys and men. Perhaps I began then to pick up the self confidence that somehow had eluded me at PA. Later, I discovered that my father had been to the recruiting station before me, had made good friends with Harris, and remained so for some time. My father loved the Marine Corps. He had seen them fight in France. To give my father credit, he chose and promoted only the best for me: Andover, The Marine Corps, and Yale. Though it was of course kept a deep secret my father loved me, too.

In compliance with Stimson's wish that we all rush to the aid of our country, (the Iwo Jima battle was going on) the school's graduation date had been accelerated, but the Marine Corps did not yet have room for me at Boot Camp, so I had an estimated two months of freedom in my new adult life. Two months is an immeasurably long time for a 18 year old, really time enough, at last, to be off and running and doing something really exciting, something you perhaps have been waiting to do for years. In fact, it was time enough, I thought, to buy an old car, get my friends together, and drive across the great, waiting continent of North America. My parents didn't think so, but to their great credit, they did not try to stop me. Maybe they knew they couldn't.

Larry was the first to heed my call and showed up at our house in Hartford with $50 bucks for the car and $50 bucks for expenses. During the week that we waited for the others to arrive, Larry and my mother discovered themselves kindred spirits and engaged in endless conversation. One time while we were washing dishes, my mother suddenly burst out laughing and said, "Wally, do you know what you are doing? About once a minute you are saying to Larry 'Keep working. Keep working.'" It was true. Larry Kohlberg couldn't stay focused on even drying a dish while his mind rushed on with manipulating transcendent abstract concepts. But his discussions on philosophy or psychology were worth it, and I liked, and he accepted, my role of keeping him working.

Larry's older sister who loved and admired him once wrote, "He tried all his life to develop more reliable motor coordination. He would have given all his academic honors in boarding school to make the baseball team, but never did. He never managed to hook a fish in Spain, go the distance in Pamplona, or keep his skis from crossing. His cars all developed battle scars front, rear, and side, before they were a week old."

One curious motor skill he tried to develop while we were at PA was slight of hand magic. He got me interested and before long we could both do the "French Drop" with consummate skill, but not much else. I still do it for kids.

By his senior year at PA Larry had developed a niche for himself, despite his total lack of athletic skills, and was well known and liked about campus. His standings in the customary student poll for seniors give some feel of how he was perceived by his fellows. He won positions in the categories of "going to seed", "unconscious", "clown", and "least civilized", but also "most sophisticated". I feel, now sixty years later and knowing a bit about Larry's life, that PA boys were not far off.

All from the rebel group at Andover, the other three passengers arrived and were Cy Chittick, the head waiter of scholarship boys and captain of the track team on which I slowly ran, Ed Wilson, a big quiet friendly boy with background in Nova Scotia who rather quickly became President of the Chicago

Board of Trade, Len Richardson, a very bright boy with a deep voice and commanding presence whom we had just elected class President, and finally myself, a newly enlisted Marine waiting to be called to boot camp at Parris Island at some unknown moment in the very distant near future.

On this, my first of many cross continental trips before the Interstates, I remember us all sleeping the night on Niagara Fall's high grassy bank just 10 feet back from the gorge and the falls, smuggling gasoline ( we had only an "A" ration card) and a huge black-market steak into the US from Canada, eating my first and best ever cheese blintz in a Jewish restaurant beneath the dark old rusty "El" in Chicago, using unrationed and dangerous naphtha dry-cleaning fluid for gasoline and, most vividly, being stopped in Omaha by a police cruiser that had been sent specifically in search of one Walter N. Morrison. This was my father again, and his new best buddy, Sergeant Harris, working together to find me. I had three days to make Parris Island.

The good cop offered to take me to the train station. His engine was idling. Dreams of driving over the Rockies and dipping the front wheels of the old Chevy into the pacific Ocean evaporated. I looked at my friends. Could I just say goodbye on a minute's notice? No one could think of anything else to say, or do, so I said goodbye. I got into the cruiser, closed the door, and the world changed.

Alone on the train, I listened to the iron wheels clanking along on the iron rails slowly but inexorably through day and night. I knew that no shortage of gas or other problem would deter my being delivered to what was now my ultimate distant and frightening destination, the Japanese Island of Okinawa. Even boot camp, six weeks, would be only a momentary stop on the way. You did not join the Marine Corps to do anything other than be a rifleman and head for the battle. A third of all the Marines that died in W.W.II had just been killed on Iwo Jima. Okinawa seemed just as bad and was a bigger island and would probably take longer. But if the battles did in fact go quickly there, it just made it more certain I would be in a landing craft, trained, armed and ready in time for the final big battle, the amphibious invasion of Japan itself.

How many people remember this prospect, this ultimate horror on our horizon? Hiroshima we remember, and rightly, but not its inevitable alternative, the invasion of mainland Japan itself. Probably no historian or military planner, or even grizzled veteran, can tell you more vividly what that invasion, assault, and battle was going to be like than the imagination of an 18 year old being trained for it as his first fight. I still have a picture in my mind of what the blood soaked, seaweed slippery, body strewn beach below the fortressed rock walls of Tokyo would look like, and what the screams and battle cries of a million Japanese defenders above, all pledged to fight to the death, would sound like. It didn't happen, but I still see it.

Half the passengers on the train were service men, going or coming, either young and fresh or old and tired. You would soon be one and look like them. The best you could hope for was that you would be like the ones coming, coming back, even if looking old and tired. You would have ribbons, like them. They had war worn seabags, stared out the windows, and smoked a lot. I bought my first pack of cigarettes and smoked. I put the opened pack and a Zippo lighter on the window ledge, like them. I chose "Lucky Strike", like theirs.

And then we got there. Yammassee, South Carolina. It is the place where shit birds get off the train, and line up straight—I SAID STRAIGHT, SHIT BIRD. YOU CALL THAT STRAIGHT. LINE UP—to march to Parris Island to begin their training. The first couple of days are designed to strip one of any sense of his individuality and to ensconce his drill instructor as God. The seriousness of this process did not totally get to me until we had to spread onto our bunks what personal belongings we had brought and watch as all items were put into trash bags and taken away. The only exceptions were bibles and rosaries, if small. I had only my toothbrush, some stamps and letter paper, and, thanks to my mother, a copy of Boethius's "Consolation of Philosophy." Not even Boethius made the cut. I felt that my very breath had been taken away from me.

But it was good. Boot camp called on my particular package of strengths and I soon knew I was doing well, despite the extreme rigors under the southern sun. I liked the rifle range and close order drill best. The latter is almost dancing, and five years later I taught my own platoon to drill with a skill they too enjoyed. (I have not naturally got quite the strength of voice that is best, so at Quantico I went out behind the railroad tracks and practiced commands with pebbles in my mouth, thank you Demosthenes.)

The earlier fire bombing of Tokyo (far more destructive than any of the more famous in Europe) had not shaken the Japanese resolve, and now, in early August, it seemed even our ultimate weapon, the Atom bomb, had likewise failed to impress or scare them. No surrender. Our platoon had only a few days of training left as early one morning we were being marched around the back bayous of Parris Island by our drill instructor, Sergeant Stengle. He had fought in every Island battle of the First Marine Division from Guadalcanal through Iwo. Now racked by persistent malaria, he had been assigned to training duty. Though one could see his body was weakened and he perspired even standing still in the shade, he nonetheless was severe and tough in his demands of us. I admired and liked him immensely. More honestly, I worshipped him.

On this morning, August 15th, as we marched along we became aware of the voice of a runner approaching and yelling at us from behind. His words became discernible first to our rear rank and then rank by rank going forward, and the great cheer went up from every throat. The wave of sound swept forward up our column to those of us in the front rank with Sgt. Stengle leading us. "The Japs have surrendered. The war is over." The message was just registering its huge import for us all when next to me the tall squad leader, Raleigh, of a southern military family, spoke out with, "Oh shit, now I won't get my chance." The next voice we heard was a great oath issuing from Stengle's throat as he lunged for Raleigh with the words, "What I'm going to give you is a chance to die, like most of my friends got." Raleigh was on the ground before he even saw the fist. Stengle marched us back to camp singing the Marine Corps Hymn and the Second World War was over for us all.

If you have ever had the chance to free a caged or trapped wild animal, perhaps a rabbit or a raccoon, see them step out of the trap, look awesomely around and maybe even at you, and then bound off with wild and weightless energy, you know how I felt after that day in August 1945. I was free. Or almost free. There was a euphoric period of a month or two while the Marine Corps caught its breath and regrouped. It even screened some of us for officer candidate school, but the trap had been sprung, I could see the open doors in front of me, and I accepted discharge in early fall. It was too late to start Yale that year. I really was free.

Larry Kohlberg lived at the end of the subway line out in Flatbush with his loving and brilliant mother, his stepfather, and siblings. I quickly found my way there. As we had hoped, Larry was also free, so we sat down and plotted what next to do. This is the way life should be. A sense that you have time and could go anywhere and do anything that strikes your fancy. For the two of us that was girls, sex, travel adventure, and bohemian intellectual life, and probably in that order. We were not being significantly financed by our families. That made the endeavors more complex, but probably more fun.

Old friend and fellow PA classmate Jack Lee had a 1930 Model A Ford roadster with a rumble seat sitting unused in Connecticut while he finished out his army time in Colorado. A deal: we could use the car if we brought it out west to him. So first—with an idea out of the blue—we would drive up to the Adirondacks and go deer hunting. Armed with a twenty gauge shotgun with slugs, a 32-40 rifle, no knowledge of hunting, and the key to Jimmy Goodwin's cabin, we took off. Discussing Larry's extensive reading of Freud (I had read only "The Interpretation of Dreams") we traversed the length and width of John's Brook valley for several days. It was beautiful, but turned very cold and snowed. To keep warm we put the two thin sleeping bags (old home made ones) one inside the other and squeezed in ourselves, but by morning concluded that we would not do that again. On our last day returning home in the dusk we were startled by three white sheeted ghosts bounding down the trail in front of us. We did not realize they were the white tailed rumps of deer until it was too late to even raise our barrels. But for consolation on driving home we ate dinner, two 18 year old boys alone with no adults, talking philosophy, at the classy Deer's Head Inn in Elizabethtown. As a scholarship boy, I had taken orders and served food for four years at PA, but I had not eaten often myself at restaurants, only diners. Larry was more cosmopolitan. Here a waitress asked our order and served us our choice, venison. To this day, when I occasionally pass this restaurant still standing 60 years later, I get a bit of the tingling, delicious, powerful feeling of first being grown up.

Back in Flatbush we prepared to drive the car west to Denver and its owner. But Larry's father, Alfred Kohlberg, suddenly demanded a visit and other doings for his son, and Larry would not be with me. A big disappointment. Alfred Kohlberg, a commanding man, was head of the Kuomintang in the US. This was a Chiang Kai Chek operation which, among other nefarious activities, ran a monopoly that controlled all the export of silk from China. Alfred Kohlberg's biography starts with a glowing introduction by Bill Buckley. I think that neither of these men would have been interested in the concept of Justice as devel-

oped in Plato's Republic which at this time was just being discovered by Larry and was to become central to his life and work.
More later.

(The following italicized section is the first of two digressions
from the main story. It's about my November road trip alone in
an open car to Denver. If you wish to get quickly to the main
story's climax, and there is one, skip this.)

*The Harrisburg-Pittsburgh turnpike had not yet been opened
through the Allegheny mountains, so with the Model A averaging
35-40 MPH over endless hill and dale it took me three days to get
to Wheeling, WV, and the flat lands beyond. But I was heading
west again, and that's where I wanted to go, have always wanted to
go, and go by driving it. There really has not ever been a driving
trip I did not enjoy, nor one I wouldn't want to start now if you
suggested it. This love began one evening in 1938 in Redlands CA
at my grandfather's house when I had been put to bed in a back
room over the driveway and garage. Having just crossed the continent by train, I was beginning to fall in love with scenery, topogra-
phy, and geography, especially of the wild and empty places. As I
was falling asleep a car arrived beneath my window and my parents and others rushed out to greet the drivers, my older brother
Frank and three friends who were completing their own first cross
continental camping trip. Their voices spoke of the exciting adventures of the open road and I knew I wanted to have them, too.*

*My brother's trip with friends was made in warm summer
weather in a 1927 Studebaker four door open touring car. I was
making my solo trip in a cold and snowy November in an open
roadster with no heater. I had not thought much about this before
starting off. In East St. Louis on a hill overlooking the Mississippi
River I made up my evening cook fire into one large enough to keep
me warm as I lay down to sleep. Shortly, two black men appeared
and asked if they could warm their hands and offered me a drink.
After a bit of friendly conversation, they gathered some more wood
and lay down to sleep. I woke early, and cold, saw an empty pint*

*bottle of Four Roses lying between my two snoring companions, put the rest of the wood on the coals of the fire, blew it alive, and left, cold but happy and heading west, across the Mississippi river.*

*Two nights later past Goodland, Kansas, with a fierce western wind blowing snow against the struggling little car, my feet got so cold I tried what I thought would surely warm them and me, but it did not. I parked the car in neutral, put the engine in idle, and lay on the ground behind the car and put my feet and slightly opened sleeping bag up against the tail pipe. I hoped that the exhaust would be warming but not deadly, given the strong wind. But by the time the exhaust traveled the distance from the engine to the tail pipe it was cold. Getting desperate, I was lucky to find that the radiator did a better job and supplied some hot water for my canteen to function as a hot water bottle. I slept till dawn.*

*The 21 inch tall, narrow, wheels of Model A Fords cut well through deep snow and get a grip on the road beneath, which is fortunate because almost to the cattle town of Limon my tracks were the only ones on the unplowed road. Unable to distinguish the road from the flat plains across which it traveled, I occasionally missed some of the right angle turns common in that country on old US Route 40 (now I 70 ). Denver wasn't much better since that metropolis had not yet stooped to snow plowing. I followed the trolley rails shining brightly through the sloppy snow through downtown to my destination.*

*Some years later Jack Lèe told me that he and wife Rosalie used the Ford for mountain ski trips and very serious courting and then decided to drive it back East. In a slow decline, the old car finally gave out for good in Hannibal, Missouri. I have written the obituaries of two other Model A's, but I like this one best. They found a city street that led straight down to the river with no barrier to the water. They took their stuff out, aimed the wheels straight down the slope, set the hand throttle up and let her go. It went straight down and plunged underwater, out of sight, thus joining the last remains of thousands of other lives sunken in the brown waters of the great*

*Missouri River. They went home on the train and soon had a new baby to play with, Virginia, who probably should have been named "Model A".*

While I had been delivering the car, Larry had found the venue for our next adventures, Bohemian intellectual life. First choice would have been London and the Bloomsbury group or Paris between the wars. But Larry had learned that we would find art, philosophy, and loose life, possibly with girls, right nearby in Greenwich Village. And we could live at his Flatbush house until we found in the village our own idealized quarters; a cramped and cold attic garret into which we would then bring a thin straw filled mattress, some broken chairs, a crooked table, art supplies, books, and a bottle of absinthe. The fact that neither of us smoked regularly, nor drank seriously, and had no art, or art supplies, did not reduce our enthusiasm a bit. Nor did we know of the existence of marijuana or "recreational" drugs of any sort, and had neither of us slept with girl or woman. An age of innocence. But it was a shared and happy characteristic of both of us to be unashamed of naivety and to be undeterred by ignorance. (Still try to be that way.) Our education was about to begin.

Minetta's Tavern on the corner of 2nd and McDougal St. (by memory) soon became the center of our wanderings as it seemed to have the mix of patron types we were looking for and the bar tender was willing to serve minors beer and food. Unknown to us there may well have been Kerouacs, Ginzbergs, or Mailers in the regular crowd we sat with, but the one name I do remember reading about in later years was Joe Gould. He was an older man with long hair and very dirty clothes. He sat every day at the bar writing on little scraps of paper, talking to himself or to anyone who would listen. There seemed to be quite a few people who wanted to listen, and buy him the next beer. To newcomers it was always revealed, as sort of the insider secret of the place, that this man was dedicating his entire life to writing the "Oral History of the World". Neither Larry or I got much out of him in his always drunken conversation, but about twenty years ago I read that the book had been published. I haven't gotten around to buying it yet.

Minetta's was a dark wood paneled smokey place with a long bar on the right and a group of tables on the left. One was round and seated about eight. This was the "regulars" table and it wasn't long before we, even though far younger than the rest, were "regulars". We were accepted partly because Larry, and to a lesser extant I, was able to keep up with conversation of the 20 to 30 year old real regulars, long term residents of the village, which focused on art and philosophy. The subjects were those that have always interested young people and have taken up so many trillions of words and arguments and are of such earth shaking importance when you first discover them: are there such things as absolute standards by which art can be judged or is it all relative and subjective? Can art be form alone or must there be content? Can art be good even if it doesn't sell? Since some of these people were trying, usually unsuccessfully, to survive by selling their work, the answer to this last one had to be "yes", by acclamation! And lets have another round of beer!

It was here in Minettas one night that we all heard Larry expound, probably for the first of many, many times in his life, on ideas from the "Republic". Plato asserted, and Larry urged, that there was an abstract Form of Beauty, the recognition of which was called Knowledge, and in contrast there were individual and imperfect manifestations of Beauty, the recognition of which was called Belief. We all fell silent and listened with appreciation, if not awe, as a curly haired youth gesturing gently with his long fingered hands spoke slowly and carefully of Socrates and Plato. At such times Larry would become so completely lost in his thoughts which were racing ahead that he might tip over a beer bottle and never notice. I loved to back him up, catch the bottle, or do whatever was needed to keep him in that amazing world of pure, abstract thought.

To help us better understand what Platonic Forms were, he might next on that night have told us of the "Allegory of The Cave". I am pretty sure I did not on first telling well understand this most famous bit of Plato, and I won't try explaining here, but Minetta's bar was a perfect backdrop for the story. Minetta's was dark, like a cave, there was the smoke and shadows as on the walls as in Plato's cave, and strongly argued Beliefs, and for one to step outside the door into the world's Reality it would be painful, and one would be disbelieved if he then reentered the cave with new Knowledge. So ever since this evening in 1945 I have had a highly personal, probably inaccurate, but very enjoyable understanding of one of the world's most powerful ideas thanks to Larry Kohlberg and Minetta's bar. Subsequent reading of the Cliff notes for "The Republic" has added only slightly to my understanding or enjoyment.

Sitting with us that night was a guy called "Big Mike' and his buddy "Little Mike". "Big" was a sculptor and "Little" a poet. Often with them at the table were two girls (I will use the terminology of the day). Though they seemed like an established foursome, the girls often gave Larry and me encouragement to talk to them more and even to sit closer to them. Elizabeth Maytag and Arcadia Bandini Mel deFontenay were twenty years old and had dropped out of Bennington College to live together in the village. They had an apartment about two blocks from Minetta's to which one evening we were all invited to go for more beer. Trading looks of excitement, Larry and I both felt that we had found our Bloomsbury or Paris, and maybe girls, too.

Climbing up the dark and dirty stairs to a grubby small two room apartment we were surprised to discover that the Mikes had not been invited to the apartment before. They, in turn, were surprised and unhappy when after more beers the girls said to Larry and me that we shouldn't try to ride the subway home that night all the way out to Flatbush but could sleep on one of their two beds. The Mikes, unhappy and jealous, got the message that they could go home to their own apartment. Larry's and my tingles of excitement were somewhat suppressed by the fact that "Big Mike" was very big, older, and clearly angry. We tried to look as innocent as, in fact, we were, and must have succeeded because the Mikes, though they grumbled their way down the stairs, threw no punches and left.

Alone with the girls with no other competing males and close to a major goal of a boys life, we were now, of course, scared and totally unsure of what to do. Fortunately the girls had an agenda, one with which we were happy to comply, even though we didn't really know what was going on. They very quickly suggested that we should the next day fetch our stuff from Flatbush and move in with them in the apartment. Grinning from ear to ear we said "sure", and we were perfectly happy to spend that night together in the front room bed while the girls slept together in the back room. There was now clearly going to be time for many nights of ecstasy in the future. Chemistry, or perhaps the girls themselves had somehow already established in Larry and my minds, without a word ever having been spoken, that the smaller, blond Elizabeth would be Larry's, and larger, dark Arcadia would be mine. We fell asleep very close to heaven, dreaming of our new possessions.

During the day we were supposed to be looking for work, and we would now need money to contribute to the rent and groceries. We had decided, again with that free ranging imagination of youth which is impossible except for the best of us to recapture in later years, that the most exciting thing we could do would be getting a berth on a merchant marine ship. As Melville asks in just the fifth paragraph of *Moby Dick* "Why is almost every robust healthy boy with a robust healthy soul in him, at some time or other crazy to go to sea?" We had spent some days quite simply walking up the gangplanks of ships moored at the various New York piers and asking if they had a job for us. This is what Ishmael had done and all the other young men of seafaring adventure stories, and it was what my great grandfather had done successfully when he was fourteen or fifteen. But in our attempt we were always turned down with little explanation. A kind but old and toothless sailor, whose envy at my eating an apple I have not forgotten, finally took us to the union hiring hall. Feeling at home with the political or philosophical position of unions, we both quickly became members of the SIU, the Seaman's International Union. But there were no ships currently in port needing crew. So it was back to Minettas and Elizabeth and Arcadia. We were happy.

We started sleeping, just sleeping, with our respective girls pretty quickly, me with Arcadia in the back room and Larry and Elizabeth on the smaller bed together in the front room. We had certainly become good friends with these girls, they seemed to very much like having us in the apartment, we got along well together, and shared a lot of interests. Though neither of them said much about it, they did not seem to have warm feelings about their families. We got the impression that the families were rich.

By agreement one night Larry and I decided we would both begin to make some overtures toward physical relationship. We had both "necked" with girls before and decided that was where we should start. Comparing notes the next morning—just a quick look was basically enough—we reported joint failure. We had been allowed to kiss them but the kisses had brought on no enthusiasm or encouragement. After a discussion alone we concluded that we had been too timid. Women must like men who are a little more confident and forward. We agreed to try that next. Remember that we had been four years at an all boys school, and sixty years ago boys had not seen the movies and television which now show youth rather explicitly what to do.

Though it was cold outside we had steam heat, but it was uncontrolled steam heat. As Arcadia and I got into bed the radiator was crackling with a new flush of steam and the room was hot and rather breathless. We turned out the light. The door between the rooms was open—the girls liked it that way—but the light was out there also. It was so warm that Arcadia and I just lay on top of the bed, I had on only my Marine Corps skivvies and she a light nightgown.

After the passage of a few minutes, with Arcadia lying on her back in the dark next to me, I threw caution to the winds and began to follow my natural urges and instincts. She did not object. While this was very exciting for me, I knew something was wrong. She seemed totally inert. I followed nature's urgings a few inches further and there was no overt backing off, but I got small subtle messages of tightening and resistance. My overtures, perhaps better called undertures, were bringing no response. I was not being welcomed. I knew if I went any further I would immediately be sent to jail for rape.

So I suffered the ignominy and pain of rejection, all of which probably would have been avoided in today's world. We would have talked, understood each other, and continued on as best friends, but not lovers. If such talking took place then, we did not know it. I listened carefully for any telltale sounds coming from the front room. The message there was also clearly, "no action."

Fortunately there was a strong winter sun coming through the smoke stained big front windows the next morning and we all woke cheerfully and had our usual breakfast in good spirits. I scrambled the eggs on the hot plate, Larry made the toast, and the girls produced the coffee and accessories. Washing the dishes in the tiny bathroom sink was always the hardest part, but always handled well by Elizabeth Maytag. The girls seemed more affectionate and attentive than ever. As best I can remember, Larry and I took our sexual rejection philosophically. Though we might previously have thought intercourse was to be the peak of our Bohemian life, we continued to enjoy the life immensely even without it. I think our ego saving rationalization was simply that these college girls felt we were too young. Our understanding of what was really going on took more time and more experience, particularly experience offered us in Paris a month or so later.

No ship wanted two totally green hands. Eventually, Larry's step father, who sold a boiler water additive called Allenite to many of the steam powered ships in the port, managed to get us each jobs, but unfortunately not on the same ship. At this time many troop ships were bringing home US soldiers and were taking German prisoners back to Europe on the return trip. We were each to be on a ship of this sort. We put a few clothes and our toothbrushes from the apartment into small canvas bags, said goodbye to each other, kissed the girls and told them we would be back in three weeks, and each headed off with our union card to our assigned ship.

At a pier on the north shore of Staten Island I found the United States Army Transportation Ship "Washington". It was unbelievably huge. I had never been close to such a big ship. I walked up the one gangplank that was down and met the officer who checked me in. "What do you want, son, the kitchen or the engine room?" I chose the engine room, having already learned from my brother how to take an engine apart and put it back together again, and I thought that might be useful. "OK, but you may end up in the boiler room as a fireman if they need you there." It turned out they always needed firemen, for good reason, so that's where I ended up, most of the time. But I didn't have to go alone.

In the little fo'castle room to which I was assigned I found Frenchie, a boisterous big hearted Canuck, Sebbie, a wizened old Portugee who loved to play cards for small stakes with younger guys relieving them only imperceptibly, but surely, of their wages, and blond Vinnie who was about sixteen but looked fourteen. At the end of the war crews of many merchant ships were very eclectic and polyglot. I remember encountering and getting to know only one professional mariner, a young officer who had recently graduated from The Massachusetts Maritime Academy and ended up urging me to try such a career. I thought about it.

I knew nothing about this interesting ship when I came aboard, and I did not learn one of the most interesting bits of history until last year, 2005, when I read *Paris 1919*. Wanting a reliable, safe, and luxurious ship, President Woodrow Wilson and his large entourage chose The "Washington", a confiscated German liner, to ferry them back and forth the several times to the Versailles Peace Conference after the First World War. The original decor was a luxurious German form of early Frank Lloyd Wright, or so I have read, but it was no longer in evidence in 1945 when I served on her and wandered the vast corridors, stairwells and dining rooms, now mess halls. In the conversion from luxury liner carrying 3000 passengers to a troop ship carrying 10,000 Mr. Wright's beautiful work had had to be dismantled. The ship was about 700 feet long, 80 feet wide and weighed 25,000 tons. It was built in 1908 for the North German Lloyd's Line in Stettin, Germany, as an entrant into that wonderful British-German competition for the the grandest ships, both battle ships, or dreadnoughts, and luxury passenger liners. The "Washington", so named in order to attract American tourists, was Germany's largest, though not fastest, ship until 1914. But—and I can't put it off any longer—most remarkable, wonderful, and exciting for me were the engines.

The 'Washington", on which I was about to make seven transatlantic trips, had the shipping world's two largest ever built reciprocating, quadruple expansion, steam engines. When I first entered one of the 60 foot high engine rooms and saw one of the warm, oil glistening, and gently breathing naked German steel

Leviathans, with a visible up and down crankshaft stroke of eighteen feet, it was for me fully the equivalent of my first visit to Chartres Cathedral. I love both visions and am not sure which one I will be seeing when I close my eyes for the last time. More later.

The "Washington" was in Hoboken, N.J. in 1914, when the First World War broke out and dared not leave for fear of capture by British and French naval vessels patrolling outside. When the US entered the war she was seized by the US and became the naval transport ship "USS George Washington". At the end of the War and after her loyal service to President Wilson in 1919, she served several different owners but was in British hands when W.W.II broke out. In 1942 the Brits gave her back to us and we refitted her with oil burning boilers—she had been coal, like most ships till then— and she then served the US Army as a troop ship in the Pacific, Mediterranean and Atlantic. I served on her in this last phase of her life. Five years later, in January 1951, she was in Baltimore and caught fire. I was then nearby in Quantico, Virginia, undergoing Marine training again and knew nothing about what was happening to my old friend. The fire completely gutted her and she was sold for scrap. I am glad I did not know at the time. Just how boats get such a grab on your heart, even that of a landlubber, I do not know. If I go to the humane society, I'm always afraid I'll come home with a dog. If I go to the James River, where today there are a lot of old ships "in storage", I would want to bring one of them home. Not a battleship, just a friendly old troopship.

(If steam engines and ship machinery bore you, skip the next three and one half pages in italics. They are written for a friend, Admiral Malcolm MacKinnon, retired Chief Naval Propulsion Engineer, for my brother, my sons, and for myself.)

*While 10,000 German prisoners filed silently on board for the next two days, I was assigned to one of the watches in the boiler room and began to learn my job. Everything on board this ship,* *from the steam tables in the kitchen, to the electric generators, to the giant propulsion engines themselves, ran on steam. So we needed steam while in port as well as when underway. But only a little bit of steam so it would be easier for me to learn my job. By memory, there were six separate boilers each with eight oil burners under them. The single oil burner in your own house furnace burns about 3/4 of a gallon of oil per hour. Each of these burners ran about 5 gallons per hour (by memory). So when 48 burners were going full blast—and it was a blast—we were putting out about the same amount of heat as 300 house furnaces. The job of a fireman was to turn burners off or on as demand for steam varied from a small amount in port to the "full speed ahead" needed when when our old ship was trying to keep up with the convoy. (There were still submarines and minefields to be avoided.) That was the easy part for a fireman. Part two was also not bad. The burner jets or nozzles had to be cleaned frequently. Turn it off and pull the burner out. Take it apart and clean the little jet hole making sure it was still sized properly, about 1/8 inch (memory). At your own home, a service man comes once a year and does this for $90. On a ship however there is an additional very hard duty for a fireman called "punching carbon". We burned bunker C crude oil, thick and dirty, and I'm sure the fire chambers and airflow were not the most efficient, thus in the fire chamber in front of each oil squirting burner a large unburned pile of pure red hot carbon would slowly build up. This would impede good combustion and heat flow up to the water tubes and could eventually choke off the fire itself. It had to be punched away.*

*There was one fireman for each of the six boilers. With the burner still firing, a twelve foot long iron rod about 1 1/2 inches in diameter weighing perhaps 20 pounds was inserted through a small hole into the fire box. The fireman, looking through another small hole, poked, thrust and wiggled the molten carbon until it broke up a bit, moved forward and started to burn. It took quite some minutes to do this for each burner two or three times on each*

6 hour watch. We were not air conditioned. The boiler room average temperature in winter was about 90 F. It was hotter up close to the burner. It was even hotter when your iron rod grew red and soft about halfway up to your hands. I have worked harder (trying to keep up with Mexicans digging sweet potatoes), but never hotter. It was still probably an easy job compared to our predecessor firemen who had steadily to shovel coal into the open doors of the furnaces.

A far more interesting and important job in the boiler room and one to which I was promoted on my last trip in June (boiler room temperature 120 F) was water tender. If the water used in making steam is not adequately replaced, the iron boiler and its tubes will be burned and melted, a disaster. Tending water means supplying just the right amount of water at the right time and under the right pressure. There were many instruments, steam pumps, and control valves involved in this job. Frenchie, the only other water tender and my teacher, could not explain in words very clearly what to do, and anyway he mostly used his own methods and a lot of intuition—sound, feel, smell, all good messengers in a boiler room. Nowadays his brain would be replaced by a computer, which might be more accurate but less colorful and less fun, and not as good at improvisation in stressful circumstances.

Frenchie was not naturally conservative but sometimes he did not trust the most important single indicator of boiler water level, the glass sight gauge mounted prominently on the front of each boiler. It does get clogged, but very rarely. Frenchie's own method when he wanted to be sure he had water was to climb 30 feet up a ladder taking with him a large soaking wet old bath towel which he would then slap up against the outside of the iron boiler about where he thought the water level was. The wet towel mark would dry immediately on the hotter iron in the steam above the water level, leaving wetness at water level and below. I am sure the methodical Germans who first ran the ship did not do it this way, but of course the Germans aren't French.

*The Germans, further, would never have allowed another Canuck (a term of endearment compared to what he called me) procedure. When we needed maximum steam production and pressure to keep up our correct position in the convoy and our boilers could not produce it, it was usually because the weighted lever arms on one of our six boiler safety valves would rise up and let steam escape (as they were supposed to do.) But with the Captain on the bridge ringing for more steam, Frenchie was always proud to produce. He simply took one or two of his supply of six brooms up onto the top of the boilers and, bracing the handle up against an overhead beam, jammed the broom down onto the offending safety valve to hold it closed. I questioned him, politely, the first time I saw him doing this. "They nevair exploding yet", was his cheerful response, and, of course, the evidence was on his side. But it was probably fortunate for The Hartford Steam Boiler Inspection and Insurance Company that I was the one who got the job with that company some years later rather than Frenchie.*

*I liked the life, the sea agreed with me, and when off watch (six on six off) I could play Black Jack with Sebbie or read a little, only a little, of Larry's loaned copy of Plato's Republic. Vinnie leaning over my shoulder one evening took one look at the sacred text and said, "No pictures?" But my favorite pastime was just prowling around all the parts of this great ship. With a little study you could figure out what everything was and how it worked. The steering was rack and pinion, just like a modern sports car. But the rack gear was a 50 foot long arc of steel fixed to the deck and the pinion gear was powered by a steam engine that moved along with the pinion as it pulled the rudder from side to side along the rack. No steam, no steering.*

*I liked to go down aft to the long narrow and deserted bays where the thrust bearings were. I never saw another person there. Each 2 foot ( memory) diameter propellor shaft, turning at 90 revolutions per minute, had a series of about ten bearing flanges, three feet in diameter around the shaft, bathed in oil in an iron cas-*

*ing. The casing was bolted strongly to the floor and hull. It was here that the forward thrust of the great propellors was transferred to the hull of the boat itself and moved us forward. I could stand there, alone, leaning on the casing, with my hand feeling the bearings inside and the thousands of pushing horsepower at work.*

*And then I could go to the ship's fantail, the lowest open deck at the stern, and watch load after load of garbage and trash being dumped overboard all day long. Men would carry it, push it, and wheel it to the edge, dump it in, light a cigarette, glance aft, look at the sky, and go back and get another load, all day, every day. The wooden crates, paper bags, cardboard boxes, tin cans, and glass bottles, that were discarded in the process of preparing food for 10,000 men three times a day, along with the garbage of uneaten food, formed a giant's Hansel and Gretel unbroken trail floating on the lonely ocean as far back as you could see behind us. Passenger Liners did this, too, but only at night under the cover of darkness. Most ships sadly, still do.*

*But the boiler and engine rooms were my favorite of all places. The whole process of turning the chemical energy of coal or oil into the heat energy of fire, and then into the potential energy of pressurized steam, and then, in the engine room, turning that steam energy into the mechanical energy of the pistons and crankshafts, which turned the propellor shafts and the propellors, all moving a 25,000 ton boat forward by pushing water back (every action has an equal an opposite reaction) was, in my discovery of it, as it was laid out so clearly and self evidently in front of me, an awesome, revelatory experience. All the important laws of physics, everything that explains the physical world to us, Newton's laws of motion, Boyle's of expanding gas, of the conservation of energy, of friction, of entropy, were there to be discovered. Even in the giant engines themselves there was not the smallest moving part or steam line valve that did not tell you what it was if you looked and thought long enough. The vertical stroke af all pistons was 18 feet, but why was the bore of the first cylinder only 3 feet and the fourth and last an astounding 12 feet? (I figure the displacement of that one cylinder alone was equal to 2,034 of Harley Davidson's biggest twin.) It was because the steam at first was high pressure and small volume and finally, after passing through 3 cylinders and having most of its energy changed into mechanical energy, it became low pressure and high volume.*

*And ruling all, of course is Entropy, "the measure of unavailability of a system's thermal energy for conversion into mechanical work: the measure of the disorganization of the universe". Oxford. All forms of energy run down hill—convert, eventually, inexorably—into heat, and can't climb back up. Simply put, that's why boiler and engine rooms are so damn hot.*

*Steam engines are not man's inventions, they are his discoveries, and make manifest the laws of nature, and are thus awesome and beautiful. The new thing of our courant age, the computer, is an invention, a design of man, and holds beauty only for such lesser, new age, beings as my older brother and my sons.*

*But enough!*

We sailed on, toward Cherbourg, my very first foreign port.

The ship slowed and I woke up early and looked out the porthole onto a sunny sea. There to the south was the pale green coast of France, sea cliffs, the skyline of a small town with no tall buildings. Close beneath my porthole a small French fishing boat was thumping along with a one lung engine. The boat had once been painted in children's bright colors, now faded and weathered with long sea-fishing use. The two man crew wore berets. A foreign port. Such a surging excitement of mind and heart had seldom hit me before and has only seldom since. I wrote a poem. I don't think this happens landing in airports.

While we sailed to ports in England and Germany also, my memories of the more frequent shore leaves in Cherbourg and Le Havre are best. The war was only a few months behind us, devastation was still everywhere, but France was still in a celebratory mood. Little cafes along the streets had plenty of what I soon learned to call "Vin Ordinaire" and of which I soon learned to drink a lot. Frenchie had friends in Cherbourg from his many previous visits and was determined to use them in helping a hesitant Vinnie overcome the impediment of virginity —-I feigned disinterest.

One day while this manly adventure was going on, Sebbie and I sat drinking at a sidewalk cafe only to be startled by a small Toonerville trolley coming around the corner and going off the tracks heading right for our table. It stopped in time. With drunken bravado and the help of some big French men and three retired (I think) professional women we pushed it back over the cobblestones and onto its bent tracks. At the invitation of the conductor, and with a hastily gathered clutch of vin ordinaire, we all took a free joyful ride around the trolley's town circuit and got back just in time to hear Vinnie's report of success. Encouraged by the buxom matrons to tell all, Vinnie was congratulated, kissed, and hugged excessively, and his story got better and better. It was as though he was at his high school graduation receiving adoring attention from his own grandmothers. I should have gone with him.

But I was the first customer of an old Frenchman who had just managed to replace the broken glass windows in his little tobacco store. He was so happy and so grateful that an American service man should be his first new customer that he didn't want to charge me for the cherry wood pipe he helped me pick out. Only because I explained the money was for his grandchildren did he finally take it.

I climbed up onto the bluffs overlooking the English Channel and saw the imposing line of concrete German bunkers that had definitely not yet been cleaned up. Looking out a firing slit, I thought again of my imagined Japanese defenders of their homeland. Had it not been for the Bomb in August it might well have been at this very moment just a few months later that Marines would have been be storming those beaches in an attempted invasion. The Japanese would be sighting their rifles down on us through gun slits just like these, and their entire population would be backing them up, which didn't happen here. I believe the bomb probably saved my life, and this belief has prevented me from ever thinking further on the subject.

Frenchie got into a bar fight one night with some local frogs. We were merchant mariners, after all! The only word we could translate in the hot argument that had started the fists swinging came out to us as "wife", but as Vinnie and I with blind loyalty attempted to back up our shipmate we both took some heavy hits. Vinnie was soon on the floor, my nose was broken and I saw more of my own blood than I had ever before or since. But, just as defeat loomed and the Military Police had been called, a few notes of La Marseillaise sung loudly by experienced Frenchie quickly turned the whole riot back into a drunken love fest.

(The French on the Normandy coast did really love US service men, and, in my experience, still do. While a group of us were finishing a country restaurant dinner there in the year 2000 the chef joined us in the dining room. With a voice full of emotion he thanked us for the Americans who had saved his and his families lives in 1945. His gratitude was so real and still so strong 55 years later he made me cry.)

"Vou le vou couche avec moi por le soir?" (This is as good as my French was then, and still is, so I leave it in its virgin state.) On the train to Paris Larry practiced repeating this classic phrase to me and I would say it back. We had had a lucky break and got leave together. I hate to think that we were less excited about seeing Notre Dame, the Louvre, or Versailles, all in our plans, but in truth I think the storied night life on a street called Rue Pigalle (Pig Alley as our Merchant Marine friends called it) beckoned most strongly. I have always known myself to have a bit of love for low life but it was, is, comforting to know that a guy with as high class a brain as Larry's had similar interests. Of course we fully expected to meet Ernest Hemingway or Gertrude Stein as we trolled the dark alleys and bright bars of the night club section, or waited expectantly to have some sort of an experience on the "left bank" that could not be hoped for on the "right bank". It was such fun to believe it could all be true. And a lot of it was.

We met good looking Yvette and Angelique early on our second morning as we were finishing up a visit to the famous old market of Les Halles. In ordering breakfast at a cafe we had become hopelessly confused with the French words for egg and water. The girls spoke fair English, helped us order, and ordered themselves. Can it happen only in Paris? Breakfast quickly became a party with the cafe staff joining in, bringing fruit, pastry, omelets, cafe au lait, and I think it must have been champagne. With the sun rising and song in our hearts, we were soon kissing Yvette and Angelique, and paying the bill. Hemingway and Stein's absence did not bother us much, particularly as the girls had begun planning a wonderful day for the four of us. The Eiffel Tower, the art galleries, lunch at La Grenouille, owned by a friend, and did we have any more of those Lucky Strike cigarettes? We did all these things and a lot more. They whisked us from bar, to store, to museum, to bar, managing always to get a cab just when we needed it, and taking complete charge of haggling for price and paying from our wallets which were the type that seamen in those days kept chained to their belts. The energy of youth, stimulated by the dynamics of two sexes, carried us on through a whole day of Parisian adventures, more than older couples could accomplish, and pay for, in a week. They had somehow sized us up as a cut above the average "sailor" and did their best to feed us with some cultural and intellectual fare, and we liked it, mostly untranslated, as much as they liked the "Luckies". They were studying, they said, at a University, not the Sorbonne, and were only a year or two older than we, they said.

We didn't slow down and ran full speed ahead into the evening. Dipping ripe fresh strawberries into cognac and then into powdered sugar and feeding the juicy lipped mouths of these girls was all I really remember of supper. But we were just a few steps away from that famous theater, the Folies Bergere, where nude models stand immobile in statuesque poses. The price in mandatory champagne per minute of bare breast was pretty high, but the show was beautiful. After this sensual warmup we were ready for the next show a few doors away down the Rue Pigalle and known as an "Exhibition", always pronounced with the accent on the last syllable. Waiting in line at the door we heard some grumbling that the show was not yet up to its pre-war quality; they had not yet found a good donkey and the trapeze did not seem to be working reliably. This, of course, only heightened our anticipation.

A Parisian "Exhibition" should not be described in words. That's why they are called "exhibitions". To be seen, only. But with some whispered explanations from Yvette and Angelique, Larry and I did learn some useful facts the knowledge of which we carried back to our apartment in New York City. The two naked girls on the stage making passionate love to each other were using an item called a dildo and they themselves were lesbians. Didn't we know? That's what you called girls that liked to live together and didn't like men in their beds but preferred to have sex with other girls. The English of Yvette and Angelique seemed to be better when discussing these subjects than it was with cathedral architecture and museum art. I whispered "Arcadia" to Larry and he whispered back "Elizabeth", and we began to suspect that our New York girl friends were thus probably lesbians. Ultimately it was satisfying to realize that our failure in bed with them was probably not, after all, our lack of manliness. That was part of what it was like to be an 18 year old boy in the days when you didn't know a damn thing. Even Larry's classical erudition had let us down. He had apparently never heard of Lesbos.

Yvette and Angelique, however, were definitely not from that island. As soon as we stepped out of the theater they led us, rather hastily, down the street and into a building that seemed to be a small hotel or rooming house. No desk or clerk. We went up the darkened stairs as two couples, and what was about to happen seemed sufficiently evident that neither Larry nor I felt it really necessary to utter our well practiced question.

Down the hall on the second floor each couple went into a room. Soon undressed and in a very comfortable bed with lots of quilts and pillows smelling strongly of perfume, our education and pleasure began. Since we compared notes in some detail afterward, I can say that both of us had a highly pleasant experience and it was with girls that we liked and who certainly liked us. It was all you could ask for.

Except for the ending. We had fallen asleep when a sudden loud banging on the downstairs door and a lot of French words yelled up the stairs woke us up harshly. Yvette, in my room, jumped up in great agitation and hurriedly threw on her clothes while telling me I did not have to do so. While barely dressed she reached for my pants and my wallet saying the hotel needed money and she took a good handful of bills and ran out the door and down the stairs. The banging and yelling had stopped. I waited. Yvette did not return. I waited some more. All was silent. She did not come back. In a few minutes I dressed and moved down the hall where I found Larry also dressing. We compared stories and found them identical. We also found that we each had only a few francs left.

Exactly what had happened we did not know. We decided to go back to our original hotel where we had spent the first night and had left our bags. We walked, to save money. We tried to figure it out. If the hotel was really after money why didn't the girls come back after paying? Maybe the girls were controlled by pimps now demanding their cut. Maybe it was all previously set up with a friend to do the knocking so they could get away with the money and back home before morning. This seemed most likely. But whatever it was, they had been great friends and bed mates while it had lasted. It was only momentarily hurtful to think that their love for us, though real, had been something less than deep, true, and permanent. Tomorrow we would find Ernest Hemingway and Gertrude Stein.

***************

My story of "Off and Running with Larry Kohlberg, 1945" ends with the mysterious departure of our frolicsome Parisian friends. Larry and I were occasionally together again in the Greenwich Village apartment with the Bennington girls, but there was no fun like Paris. We did learn that Elizabeth was a real Maytag and I later learned in California that the Bandinies owned large chemical and fertilizer companies. These girls, Lesbian or not, had been good friends for us and we, in turn, had supplied them with a cover story they apparently felt they needed in 1945. Whether they are still alive or not I do not know.

Larry and his troop ship went on to engage in smuggling Jews from Europe into Palestine through the British blockade. Larry had a prominent personal part in successfully convincing the British port inspectors that the large boxes in which the jews slept were actually banana crates.

He subsequently went to the University of Chicago and then Harvard where he became quite famous as a psychologist and philosopher. In addition to Plato, Larry was inspired by Dewey and Piaget. He is best known for his theory on the six stages of moral development and for starting several of Plato's "Just Communities" in schools and prisons. TIME magazine called him a "seminal thinker". If you put "Lawrence Kohlberg" into Google or Wikipedia you will have interesting reading.

# Off and Running with Larry Kohlberg

************

Larry died by suicide in 1987. He had picked up a tropical parasite and had never been able to get it out of his system despite increasingly heavy doses of medication. The parasite, or too much medicine, gradually ruined his body and warped his mind. A tough way to go.

Finally I include some of Larry's own writing as the best way to get a feel of the man. The words are his own brief statement of the six stages of moral development and were included in a 1970 book the cover of which I also reproduce.

Thanks, Larry, for the fun friendship of our youth and for some mental furniture that has enriched my life.

A Harvard Paperback / $2.95

**Five Lectures by
James M. Gustafson
Richard S. Peters
Lawrence Kohlberg
Bruno Bettelheim
Kenneth Keniston
on**

# Moral
# Education

**With an Introduction by
Nancy F. and Theodore R. Sizer**

Because morally mature men are governed by the principle of justice rather than by a set of rules, there are not many moral virtues but one. Let us restate the argument in Plato's terms. Plato's argument is that what makes a virtuous action virtuous is that it is guided by knowledge of the good. A courageous action based on ignorance of danger is not courageous; a just act based on ignorance of justice is not just, etc. If virtuous action is action based on knowledge of the good, then virtue is one, because knowledge of the good is one. We have already claimed that knowledge of the good is one because the good is justice. Let me briefly document these lofty claims by some lowly research findings. Using hypothetical moral situations, we have interviewed children and adults about right and wrong in the United States, Britain, Turkey, Taiwan, and Yucatan. In all cultures we find the same forms of moral thinking. There are six forms of thinking and they constitute an invariant sequence of stages in each culture. These stages are summarized in the table.

Levels and Stages in Moral Development

| Levels | Basis of Moral Judgment | Stages of Development |
|---|---|---|
| I | Moral value resides in external, quasi-physical happenings, in bad acts, or in quasi-physical needs rather than in persons and standards | *Stage 1:* Obedience and punishment orientation. Egocentric deference to superior power or prestige, or a trouble-avoiding set. Objective responsibility |
| | | *Stage 2:* Naively egoistic orientation. Right action is that instrumentally satisfying the self's needs and occasionally others'. Awareness of relativism of value to each actor's needs and perspective. Naive egalitarianism and orientation to exchange and reciprocity |
| II | Moral value resides in performing good or right roles, in maintaining the conventional order and the expectancies of others | *Stage 3:* Good-boy orientation. Orientation to approval and to pleasing and helping others. Conformity to stereotypical images of majority or natural role behavior, and judgment by intentions |
| | | *Stage 4:* Authority and social-order maintaining orientation. Orientation to "doing duty" and to showing respect for authority and maintaining the given social order for its own sake. Regard for earned expectations of others |
| III | Moral value resides in conformity by the self to shared or shareable standards, rights, or duties | *Stage 5:* Contractual legalistic orientation. Recognition of an arbitrary element or starting point in rules or expectations for the sake of agreement. Duty defined in terms of contract, general avoidance of violation of the will or rights of others, and majority will and welfare |
| | | *Stage 6:* Conscience or principle orientation. Orientation not only to actually ordained social rules but to principles of choice involving appeal to logical universality and consistency. Orientation to conscience as a directing agent and to mutual respect and trust |

# WAR STORIES

I served in Korea as a junior Marine Corps officer from November 1951 through August 1952 leading the 2nd rifle platoon of Howe Company, 3rd Battalion, 5th Regiment of the 1st Marine Division. We were on the front lines, mostly in the mountainous eastern flank, and were occasionally in regimental reserve. During this period of the war there were no great battles, advances or breakthroughs. I led reconnaissance and harassing patrols in no-man's land in front of our lines, mostly at night, and guerrilla searching patrols in rear areas. We did have occasional brief fire fights with North Koreans and Chinese, took incoming mortar and artillery rounds, and struggled to avoid land mines, but none of my men were killed and I was not wounded. I know that I was lucky in Korea. I also am proud to have served well in this most illustrious Regiment and feel comfortable that even though it would now be crowded with many others there is a place for me there leading my old platoon should I ever in the end want to go.

I feel warmly about the Marine Corps partly because of an officer for whom chance assigned me to work when I returned as a Private to the Corps in late 1950. Wallace Martin Greene, Jr. was a native Vermonter and was then a Colonel in the Marine Corps Schools at Quantico. I became, of all improbable things, his Clerk, and ran all his office functions except stenography. He was reserved, of course, humble, smart, fair and hard working. Only your intuition and his ribbons could tell you how much steel and ambition were also in this somewhat small and quiet man. I did not come to worship him as I had my Parris Island drill instructor 6 years earlier, but I certainly admired him a great deal and eagerly did all the extra jobs he gave me from editing and indexing a secret manual for an early electromechanical shipboard gun aiming computer (yes, I did it) to serving cocktails at his home parties. I may be a controlling type, but give me a leader I can admire and I will happily follow and help him anywhere. And I had chosen well in admiring Greene. He soon became Commandant of the Marine Corps Schools, then Commandant of The Marine Corps itself, and a member of the Joint Chiefs of Staff. He was my mentor, got me commissioned from the ranks, a "mustang", as the Marines call it, and urged me to consider the Corps as a life career. Had I done so, and I certainly considered it, my way would probably have been well paved by him.

One of my men did a skillful pencil sketch of me leading the platoon over some rough terrain in Korea. I sent it to my father and he sent it to Colonel Greene.

My father received a letter in return:

Dear Mr. Morrison,

Thank you for sending me the copy of the pencil sketch of "Marines on the March!" I think that the drawing is a small indication of the type of Lieutenant your son is. What his platoon thinks of him in the field is a good gauge. Enlisted men make few mistakes in taking the measure of their leaders - and what they evidently see in Morrison is also what I saw when he came to work with me here in Quantico. His ability and integrity reflect the care his father and mother have given him. I hope that he decides to make the Marine Corps his career......I am being transferred. Perhaps I shall see him again soon.

Sincerely yours,
Wallace Greene, Jr.
Colonel, U.S.Marines

*************

So where are these war stories? One source is the letters I wrote home at the time, but I had not looked at them until sitting down to write this. I have now found and read many of them. Strangely, they do not focus on the half dozen or so specific scenes or events that have lived most actively in my memory for 55 years, and further, they do describe a lot of events and people I don't now remember. Some of the memories that have vividly survived are poignant, some scary, some disturbing and sad. They prove, for me anyway, Ezra Pound's dictum "only emotion survives."

***************

I had been in charge of my platoon for only a few weeks and we had moved up into a defensive position on the very top of hill 854 (meters). It is late December, very cold, with a lot of snow and wind. The moon is bright. After the rather terrible anxiety and anticipation of taking over one's first command and facing the enemy, I am just beginning to get comfortable with my role and job. (In this particular environment I have significant help from my previous experience in winter mountaineering.) I have led two patrols—no enemy contact— out through the barbed wire down into the no man's valley lying between us and the Chinese. Each time we leave or reenter the wire our route takes us past a dead and frozen Chinese soldier facing up hill hunched over on his knees just outside our perimeter. On returning up the long ridge at the end of the second patrol I am saying to myself "I can do this" and feeling good. At the wire I turn and look hard at the frozen soldier and wonder about him for the first time. Some of my men talk with me about him. He must have been shot by the troops we had relieved and then was just left here. I am curious. The man seems to be carrying a bundle, his chest now humped over it. I go over to inspect him, but am warned by a smart private to look out, he might be booby trapped. We get a long stick and tip the man over. I feel that my men are sizing me up as OK. At least I am not afraid of a Chink who is already dead. Maybe I was planning on this. Concluding he is safe we study the bundle and then open it. The moonlight is strong enough for us to see that inside the wrapping there is a large stack of folded paper cards. We look harder and closer. They are Christmas cards. Christmas cards for us from the Army of the Chinese People's Volunteers, brought to us by this man. I think we were quiet for a moment, or two, but then somebody said "Just in time for Christmas, three days." We all took a couple of cards. I did not take one of the cards with his blood on it.

When I have looked at this card and its message, now among old souvenirs, I know that its purpose was to undermine our will to fight, but I always wonder, and wonder again, did this Chinese man volunteer for this job? Was he a true believer in communism, the justness of the Chinese cause? Or was he just a humble obedient soldier? It seems to me, however, that really almost any man not volunteering, but ordered by his commanders to go, would merely have moved out toward our position and then dumped the cards at some safe distance below our lines in the snow under a tree, then gone back to his side and reported the mission accomplished. No one would ever know. But here he was. He had climbed up the long snowy ridge, alone, in the cold moonlight, carrying his heavy bundle of Christmas wishes, wishes for peace and the war's end, and brought them to our lines. To have made the unnecessary struggle and to face the deathly risk, this man had clearly believed in something. Was he a true believing Christian? That, too, could move a man. Would I be easier knowing what he was, what he had believed? Would I be easier had I not so eagerly tipped him over with the long stick. Why did I do it? It might have been better if I had just left him alone, as everyone else had. Found no Christmas cards.

To give myself consolation, consolation for something, to pay for something, I have allowed and maybe even encouraged the image of this man, huddled, frozen, dead, to come alive in my mind, for 54 years now, at Christmas time. Turns out he was a booby trap after all.

************

Sarah and I sleep in a double bed, and sometimes I wake up early in the morning and am lying on my back. I look over and see Sarah in the same position. We are warm and comfortable, side by side. I lie there waking up slowly. We have a large skylight over the bed. Sometimes it is so pleasant that I would like to lie there forever, just watching the sky lighten with the dawn, watching a cloud or two pass, and waiting for the gulls and crows to come flashing quickly overhead on their way to finding an early breakfast. I say to myself, "Life could not be better."

I also think of another couple, Koreans, long ago, once lying in this position, and wonder what their feelings were. Surely sad. But they were old and maybe ready to die. Wanted to stay in their house. They could have left with everybody else.

The village was larger than others we had checked out. Maybe two or three streets and 20 or so buildings. The houses were more substantial, not big, but some made of stone and mortar. We had hiked in fifteen miles through a fresh snowfall and would be picked up by helicopter. But it soon was clear to us that we weren't going to have any trouble. No tracks or signs of life anywhere. As the men checked on through the houses I moved ahead with Corporal Nichols to the farther end of the village up on a little rise. One house there looked a little more important than the others.

Before entering the house we stopped to study the outside part of its heating system. We were beginning to understand how these worked. Outside, at ground level on the lowest side, there was a stove-like fireplace up against the mortar wall of the building with the flue leading directly under the masonry ground floor. The flue divided into a web of channels and carried the hot smoke under a large section of the floor and ended up at the chimney on the far side of the house. We never actually saw one working but our Korean interpreter said that a good wood fire really warmed the floors up and heated the whole house.

Nichols opened the big wooden door and we went in. The first room was apparently the kitchen and dining-living room. There was a table and utensils and a cupboard, but not much else. There were no chairs. It seemed a little barren and we surmised that the owners had taken away some furniture with them.

I entered the second room ahead of Nichols. I saw a man and a woman lying neatly on their backs side by side facing me on the bare floor. They were dead. They had probably been dead for some time, but because of the cold and freezing they still looked normal. The man had a thin white beard and the woman's face was wrinkled. Though their clothes were now shapeless on their bodies I believe they were fairly fancy clothing of the type that drapes well in hanging off the shoulders. Both of them seemed to have on many layers of material. They each held their bare hands crossed on their chests.

With Nichols looking on I knelt down beside the woman. I tried moving her arm a little just as a test of her condition. It was stiff and frozen. It was a small, frail, body, and the skin of her hands and face was very wrinkled. The expression on her face was, if it was anything, peaceful. I guessed that she was very old. Under her hands I noticed a little round bag strangely made of bits of cloth, thread, string, and fiber. I remember thinking it looked like a Baltimore Oriole's nest. I gently held it up, and asked myself out loud, "Should I open it?" Behind me Nichols mumbled some agreement and I began to open it. It was very much like a nest. Inside was a tiny pair of scissors, a paper packet of needles, and some spools of thread. Also there was a small brown paper booklet with a tiny picture of a woman and some Korean script and numbers. Probably an identification card. Finally, in a miniature frame the size of a postage stamp was an old sepia brown picture of a young Korean man. Nichols was now down beside me on his knees. Clearly moved, as was I, he said something loving about mothers, and grandmothers, but so softly I didn't, and didn't need to, understand him. We put the items back in the bag and I put it under her hands again.

I turned to look at the husband. He had on a stiff black hat that supported his head a bit off the floor. His face had a natural look, perhaps also peaceful, but the faint expressions could be due to freezing. There was no way to know. A small collection of building tools lay on the floor behind his head. I remember a saw, the first Oriental pull-type blade I had ever seen. His hands and fingers were very twisted and claw-like with age as they lay crossed over his chest. He had nothing under his hands, but on the floor beside his waist was a small carved, curious, wooden device. It had a turning metal axle at one end with a string on it. I did not figure out until some years later that it was a carpenter's chalk line, but it appealed to me and it is now on the bookshelf beside me as I write. I, too, became a carpenter and have my own chalk line as well as his.

We stood up and gave one last reverential look at this ancient husband and wife, lying neatly in their death on the slowly cooling, now cold, floor after their last fire, the wood all used up, in the house where he had been the craftsman and she the housekeeper for so many years, side by side.

As we stepped outside, some of the other troops were just approaching. Nichols slammed the door hard behind us and yelled out in his loudest corporal's voice, "Nobody in here, guys, move on."

\*\*\*\*\*\*\*\*\*\*\*\*\*\*

Since it probably was about as close to being hit by a bullet as I ever came, I have thought that if I told this story it would show fear and that I was scared, and maybe I really was. But memory is smarter than we are and it fools us in order to provide what it knows we need. I don't remember scary. I remember camaraderie and funny.

It was a daytime patrol heading down into the valley in deep, new snow. A full squad of men, all wearing our new white camouflage clothes. About halfway down the hill rifle fire suddenly cracked out from the ridge on our left, about 3 or 4 hundred yards away. Most of our men immediately jumped to the right side of our ridge and were in a safe position from which to return fire, but a few were caught too far down the left flank and had to hide behind bushes and rocks. It was hard for either side to see targets well and the range was such that only an expert could hit somebody. But sporadic firing went on for some minutes.

Along with Grant Vickers, our telephone wire man, I was near the rear of the squad. When the distances weren't too great we were required by our Battalion Commander to carry a heavy reel of phone wire with us, unreeling as we went, and to periodically report in to him on our sound powered telephones. It is true that in this way we could call in mortars or other support but most of us, platoon leaders, had become unhappy with the way some senior officers used the phone to try running our show which we, on the ground, could run better. Whenever our Colonel, whose immediately previous command had been, tellingly, the Portsmouth, N.H. Naval Prison, the Brig, heard any firing he would immediately get on the phone and want to know what was happening. We dared each other to say some prisoners were escaping. But didn't.

Grant and I had dropped over the right side of the ridge. Grant, a dutiful and technically oriented young man, who was also very tall, had quickly connected the phone and had just spoken to our Captain who, of course, wanted to know, before the Colonel did, what the hell was happening. Mistakenly believing that we were in safe defilade, Grant and I were both standing up. Grant had the phone pressed to his ear, I was looking at him, standing slightly above me, with my hand out waiting for him to hand me the phone so I could report. At that moment the receiver of the phone exploded in Grants ear. With a startled look of total dismay Grant glanced at the receiver and then collapsed straight down into the snow. I did, too. Looking, I could see blood in a slight crease on Grant's skull that ran directly through the lobe of his ear and I knew what had happened. But as he continued to look at the receiver, Grant said, "How can that happen? It can't explode." I told him a bullet had nicked him and shattered the receiver. He put his hand up, felt the cut scalp and ear and saw the blood. The dismay left his face but was replaced by an impossible combination of fear and relief. I thought he might pass out, but in a moment he smiled at me and said, "I knew there's not enough voltage in these phones to explode!"

Under cover of some steady fire from our men, our exposed Marines made a successful dash for the back side of our ridge and all started to move back up the hill. The Chinese moved back downhill behind their ridge. They had accomplished their mission of harassing us; we had accomplished ours of letting them know they could not do it with impunity. Next week the roles would be reversed and that was a lot of what took place in the middle year of the Korean War. In the meantime I had failed to report 'what the hell was going on" to either the Captain or the Colonel.

The Captain, just newly arrived and still mostly unknown to us, was waiting for us as we reentered our lines. When I told him what had happened with Grant and the phone he said, "The Colonel is not going to believe this, Morrison, and I'm not sure I do. I'll have to see this phone."

When Grant was finished pulling in and reeling up the wire he came over with the phone. Holding it in his hand the Captain studied it and glanced at Grant's ear, but gave us no clue to his reaction but for a slow and quietly uttered "Jesus."

His posture and expression then changed a little in a way that somehow gave me confidence that he was a cool old timer. Addressing Vickers in a strong voice he said, "Morrison tells me you are a good Marine, Private Vickers, but the evidence here in my hand tells me you are a little careless. In the old Corps when I was a private if you let the enemy destroy government property it was a court martial offense. Nowadays, I suppose, if you just pay for this phone yourself it will probably be OK—"

I have never been sure, because the Captain continued talking, but I think I heard Grant say, in his dutiful way, "I'll pay, sir".

"—-and this evening the other officers and I will have a meeting and discuss whether to recommend that you be awarded the traditional Purple Heart or whether you should be the first to receive the newly established Order of the Purple Ear." Turning to me he said gruffly, "As for you, Lieutenant, you will lead tonight's patrol also unless you can get one chicken shit Colonel off my back. He's waiting on the phone line in my bunker. Waiting. Good luck. I'll go help your Corpsman patch up Grant's ear."

*****************

Corporal Arnold Hungerford was a young man who had been happily addicted to the technology of firearms since he got his first Marlin 22 caliber rifle in childhood back in Iowa. He loved the smell of Hoppe's gun oil, the hidden explosive power in one small measure of gunpowder, the beauty in a precisely filed trigger sear. He had no violence in him and was not really interested in guns as instruments to kill people, but he knew the grains of powder and grams of bullet weight for every caliber and load. Most of all he was fascinated by the mathematics of muzzle speed and trajectories of different weapons. He would have had a good time with my brother and father.

When I first took over the platoon and we moved up on line I had been surprised to see that he and the other two members of his fire team were carrying extra weapons. One was a light weight air cooled Russian Machine gun on a bipod mount and also, of all incredible and romantic weapons, a 45 caliber Thompson sub machine gun with the large drum magazine. How it made it from the 1930s streets of gangland Chicago to Korea no one knew. He also carried his standard issue Garand M1 rifle, and was a good shot. I accepted Arnold and valued him though he was known for being late, sloppily dressed, and sometimes resentful of, if not resistant to, military authority.

Because he could get no ammunition for the Russian gun, as he explained it to me one day, he had traded it for a damaged US 50 caliber machine gun and a belt of ammo that had been salvaged from a rolled over and crashed Dodge Power Wagon. By now I knew enough not to ask him any questions about how, when, or where this transaction had taken place and he knew I wouldn't. The excitement was that 50 calibers were supposed to have an effective range of over 1000 yards, compared to the Garand's 500 yards. He had managed to get the dirt out of the bore and the action, bent the cooling shield back to where it belonged, and had the weapon apparently ready to fire. He now needed my permission to go behind the lines somewhere and test it and sight it in. I did grant this permission, willingly, and from here on in I became his accomplice and abettor. I wish I hadn't.

Just forward of the very peak of our mountain there was a bunker we had built for the occasional naval gunfire and artillery observer. Sitting on its flat sandbagged roof we had our best view of the enemy ridge line and the valley between us. We had all noticed that the Chinese had a diagonal gully behind which they could descend to the valley floor more safely than any way we could. We also thought that they sometimes camped overnight at the foot of the gully and stayed there between several patrols. We carefully estimated the range of this spot to be 800 yards. Taking turns studying the area for long periods of time through our pair of 7X50 binoculars we sometimes saw a man in the morning make the short round trip out of the gully shelter over a dirt bank down through the brush of the valley floor with what looked like a bucket. We assumed he was going for water.

Behind the lines Arnold successfully test fired the 50 caliber as a single shot rifle and sighted it in at 800 yards, using some abandoned oil drums as his target and a friend with a phone line as his spotter. The two of us then spent some time computing how much to lower the rear sight to compensate for the 1200 foot down drop of the trajectory. We then built a very solid sand bag rest on top of the observation bunker so we could sight the weapon with absolute steadiness.

Despite the exposure of the location, several other Marines had slipped in to watch our attempt to spot and catch the water bearer. Word had spread. I don't think we thought we could really pull this off, but the preparation for and the anticipation of the attempt had preoccupied us happily. This excitement was despite the fact that at this early spring date in 1952 each warming day brought renewed rumors of a cease fire hopefully soon to come.

But we had to try.

The rifle was sighted in at the upper end of the dirt bank just where we knew the man would pass. Arnold suggested I be the one to shoot, but I deferred to him. I think I thought he was really just being deferential to his officer, and I was proud to be the kind of officer that put his troops desires first. But I didn't really know myself well enough then, and don't now, to be sure why I declined.

Arnold lay down in a good prone position and put his eye on the sights and his finger on the trigger. All we had too do now was to wait until the man came and then Arnold would pull the trigger. We must have waited for a long time but all I remember was a clear sunny day. I don't remember the waiting. Then suddenly we all did see the man, always young in my mind but this has to be imagination since there is no possible way I could tell at that range. You could see him make the move even without binoculars. Arnold's shot rang out. We saw the young Chinese soldier cartwheel down the bank into the brush below. I don't remember any cheers, but there may have been cheers. I just remember Arnold as I turned to look at him in his prone position saying, "Shit." He raised up on his elbows still looking at the target and said "shit" again. Without looking at any of us, as if we weren't even there, he got up, said it again, and walked away by himself over the path to the rear of our lines.

# KOREAN ADDENDUM

In some way my "paperwork skills" became known to the Colonel commanding our 3rd Battalion and I was ordered to duty as his S-1 officer—Adjutant, Legal, Personnel, Administration, etc. I did not much like the Colonel, and I did not like the work, and I missed my platoon. Actually I felt more worried and scared about getting hit by something, a stray artillery shell, than when I was with my platoon. I think this feeling is common with young officers who have literally fallen in love with their command. When you are with your men you are invincible and feel you can do anything, and for them, you will also do absolutely anything. With important symbolism, Marine officers when in the field with their troops eat at the end of the chow line, after the troops have had what they want. These feelings are so strong and sustaining that you don't worry too much about getting hit yourself.

But after a month or so as Battalion S-1 Officer, the message arrived one spring day that the Lieutenant who had taken over my old platoon had been seriously wounded and had been evacuated. I expressed my worry and anxiousness about the leaderless platoon to the tight-lipped savvy old Battalion Sergeant Major, who was my "assistant". He responded, rather casually, that if I really wanted to I could just go, leave headquarters now, and rejoin the platoon on the line. Puzzled, I asked about the Colonel. With 25 years of experience behind him the Sergeant responded, "Sir, no one will ever question a Marine about obeying orders or anything else as long as he is moving forward. I'll take care of the Colonel and the paperwork." So, wisely allowing myself no moment for reflection, I quickly spoke the only words of response possible to the Sergeant's statement and said, "I'm going." As we parted, the Sergeant said with carefully measured pride and satisfaction, "That's the way the old Corps always worked", and then, bringing his eyes back from their distant gaze to the front, and with summoned new energy he awarded me a sharp salute. Like all the best of his rank he knew how to manage and train new Lieutenants, and I suspect a few Colonels, too.

My memories of leading the platoon for the the next months in spring and early summer cannot really be fully accurate, but I have them and enjoy most of them a lot. The Marine Division had moved over toward the West Coast and our particular section was low, rolling, open hills, pleasantly grass covered, with a few low flat places of rice paddies. In my memory we were a totally detached and separate unit reporting in to no one and just wandering about the country side helping out where we could. Infrequently it was bad. Once, moving forward along the raised edge of a rice paddy to back up some Republic Of Korea troops, three mortar rounds came plunking quickly down into the paddy so perfectly placed and so close to us—and my fault to have us so close together— I was sure we were all going to die. I could see the explosions under the deep mud bursting up and looking like high speed photos of raindrops hitting water. In the second or two while I was trying to make gravity pull me more rapidly down to the ground I foresaw the whole gruesome tragedy coming to us, and after so much luck. My emotions of that moment remain wrapped in a tight ball. But for some unknowable reason the mortar rounds went down so deep into the mud that all their energy was absorbed by it, thus leaving practically harmless the little shrapnel that actually reached us. As was the mud. We then ran forward so fast, very fast, there was no danger from the next three rounds which landed right on the path where we had been. We got to the ROK troops just in time to team up with them. With our combined firepower we helped push the MLR forward four hundred yards. This was possibly, I suspect, one of the more measurably "useful" things I helped do in Korea. Who knows?

We had found a huge piece of canvas and took it with us as we moved and at night made a giant center pole Arab tent with it. Many days we just lay in the sun warmed grass or under the shade of the tent and talked and rested. After the cold dark mud bunkers of the frozen winter this was great luxury. The tent, in reality, was probably only twelve or fifteen feet in diameter, but it was large enough to shelter my now large "headquarters gang." In the gang, along with me, there were;

Sergeant Lou Mesics. My senior enlisted man, about 25, totally competent and loyal and good-natured. He returned to a career in prize fighting when the war was over. He died just a while ago.

A Navy Medical Corpsman. Can't remember his name. Gentle, fearless, and always tending closely to us. Fortunately we never saw him have to perform the really hardest stuff but we knew he could have.

Radio Man. In our detached duty we had been supplied with what then passed as a mobile radio. It was a full heavy backpack load for one man and worked only erratically. Diego, from Puerto Rico, carried it and operated it better than the rest of us, but there was a problem; Diego didn't speak great English. That I spoke some Spanish helped, a little.

But I spoke no Korean or Chinese. So we had been assigned an interpreter. Lee (let's call him) was a young Korean, maybe 20 years old, from Seoul, an educated city boy. His English was about as good as Diego's. We finally captured one prisoner and were supposed to immediately transmit information from him to headquarters. I had trouble getting Lee's halting English translation of the prisoners Korean words into an English that Pedro could understand and then transmit it to the radio operator in headquarters who was, of course, totally unfamiliar with Spanish. Laughter ensued and I think even the prisoner smiled.

Sitting around a small and sheltered campfire on the last night I was with the Platoon, Lee broke his usual reserve and wanted to talk. He wanted to know the answer to the big question. Why was I fighting in Korea? He startled me. It was a question I hadn't asked for a long time. Most of us, Marines, resolved the issue with the appealingly simple and age old statement that we were fighting for the Corps and its honor and to support our buddies. It was a genuine feeling. But I doubt if it was an answer that satisfied Lee. And in view of what he confided to me it became even less likely to satisfy either of us. He told me that his father was a high official in the Bank of Korea who was helping President Singman Rhee transfer $60 million dollars to Rhee's personal account in the Philippines. Totally unexpected, far-out and dramatic as this revelation was, I believed Lee. And sure enough I later saw this fact along with Rhee's desertion of Korea reported in the newspapers. I should have asked Lee why *he* was fighting. His personal reserve until this, our last night, prevented us from sharing what I suspect was the case—neither of us really had a strong, or strongly rational reason why we were there. How many soldiers do? Rationalization abounds, but is not reason.

Runner. I don't know if the infantry still has or uses runners, but we did. When phones or radios fail, you sent a runner. Gonzales, a rather chubby Mexican, was our runner. I don't think we ever had to send him anywhere with a desperate message, but he was helpful with the tent, firewood, water, food stolen from the Army, making sure we got our full ration of Asahi Beer, and other high priority items.

Finally, a House boy, Han. Han was about 14 and had just shown up out of nowhere one day. A healthy, but thin, classic looking Korean boy with a good smile, no parents, and minimal clothing and shoes. With great canniness he first ingratiated himself with Gonzalez by helping quietly and efficiently with his tasks. Like kids anywhere with any brains and serious motivation he learned in no time to speak our language—that is languages, both Spanish and English. (In contrast, and despite efforts, I learned perhaps five Korean words, remembering now, 55 years later, only two or three: scoshi, meaning little, and wamba-da, a favorite of joking Korean men, meaning cuckold. My survival did not depend on quick learning as perhaps Han's did.)

Man by man Han worked his way up our hierarchy until he got to where I am sure he had been aiming right from the beginning, namely me. And I was a pushover. He tried to anticipate my every need and was usually successful. He slept curled up at my feet. And as with a dog living with a group of tough men, it was OK to show affection for him, and we all did. With our food he began to gain weight immediately. Some guys even sewed clothes for him. My mother sent him a red flannel shirt. History says we were really only continuing a tradition of military officers and sea Captains having house boy assistants or cabin boys. I think my great grandfather's first trips to sea at age 13 may have been in this role for Commodore James Biddle on whose ship he sailed. For the right kid—include me in—it would be a great start in life.

Instead of the Halliburton Company supplying all our logistical needs for the transport of food and ammunition to forward positions, we had battalions of Korean laborers who carried everything to us in immense loads on their backs. They were frequently older, wonderful men and I liked them a lot. One of them taught me how to Indian wrestle so skillfully that I have seldom been beaten ever since. They were called "Chiggi Bearers".

Shortly before I finally left the platoon, Han inveigled me into going with him to the Korean Labor Camp where that evening a Korean play was being performed. I could not understand a word, but enjoyed listening to the audience and Han laugh. I was the only US person there. It was two hours long, on a hard wooden bench. But I got a surprise reward the next day when every Korean laborer in camp saluted me.

Before I could ship out for home, I did duty for a month running part of the defensive perimeter around, and protecting, division headquarters (where I found many officers had house boys.) I had been considering becoming a regular Marine Corps career officer—as well as being a logger, mountain climber, school teacher, hobo and several other now long forgotten life alternatives. But here in Headquarters the Marine Corps seemed to lose its attraction. Maybe the General, the leader of us all, felt as supported by, and as affectionate towards, his 10,000 men as I had for my six man headquarters and 42 man platoon, however I began to realize that for me a Division was too big, abstract and impersonal to imagine enjoying it or any military life at the upper levels, especially in peacetime. Running a Division requires Professional *Management* of the sort required in a business organization. I can and have enjoyed that, but much less so than the informal personal *Leadership* of all the men in a unit. Perhaps I am intimidated by size—-I enjoy small business companies, small towns, more than large—-but I think it is really more a matter of enjoying the close personal relations and ego strokes of leadership in small groups more than the particular type of ego trip granted by bigness and which is generally considered the pinnacle of success. Further, I had recently read T.E. Lawrence's (Lawrence of Arabia) "War in the Desert" and was probably spoiled for the appeal of anything less powerful and romantic. So, though I was glad to be soon going back to the States, here in Headquarters I began to feel a little let down in my love affair with the Corps as I slowly realized she was not going to be my life partner. The let down was really pretty big.

There was one thing, however, I did like at headquarters and that was the parades with a strong Marine Corps Band with lots of drums playing Sousa. The officers and NCOs in Headquarters Company run the Division level parades, and with very significant help from an old Gunnery Sergeant I had performed my part well in passing us all in review when some Army big wigs were visiting. (Was it Ridgeway?)

A week or two later good Bob Hope came and gave us a great show. On the next day we were going to give him the best parade we could. That morning the old Gunny, with whom I was tenting, had joined me in opening a "care" package from friend's mother back home. It was a giant size cylindrical Quaker oatmeal box packed with chocolate chip cookies and, hidden in the center, a bottle of Gin, totally unknown in Korea. You can see what's coming, but I didn't. I had errands to do and I left the Gunny and the package alone for too long. When the time came for him to be dressed and ready to run the parade—and he was the one who really knew what to do, I just looked good and yelled a few orders—- the Gunny was smashed. He kept urging me to have a little drink myself and we would then both get through with this parade for Hope and nobody would ever know. Well, we almost did.

As we started off he had a good loud voice, sounded like he knew what he was saying, and the troops and I knew more or less what to do. But this parade required some fairly precise maneuvering because our parade field had been scraped out of a hillside and was small and curving in shape. There was a point at the end of the field when the Gunny had to walk backwards facing his troops. Suddenly, carrying his long and impressive marching parade staff, he and his resonant voice disappeared backwards over the edge and down the bank. Fortunately, before I had to say a word, the Sergeant from the nearest platoon stepped out and took the Gunny's place and we carried on having missed only a few noticeable beats. But you can imagine who was smiling and who wasn't when we passed the reviewing stand.

I had been flown to Korea in November of '51, making 5 stops for fuel and repairs on an old Navy R4D, and could have flown home now in the fall of '52, but there was a need for an officer to accompany returning troops on a ship back to San Diego. I wanted to be with the troops again. So I volunteered. I crossed a new ocean, the Pacific, on a troop ship, and this time I was a passenger, not in the Merchant Marine crew as I had been on the Atlantic in 1945 and '46. Back in California at Camp Pendleton I was soon released from active duty, have no medals for personal valor, but do have six theater or campaign ribbons with three battle stars for events that took place while I was in Korea. (Same as my father in World War 1.) Later, in 1960, I resigned from the Marine Corps Reserve as a Major, fifteen years after my first enlistment. My serial number was 053007. It was a good experience for me.

***********************

I think that there is permanently in our genes from back when we were a pack of animals, or primitive men, a drive to and pleasure in being a member of a group of men with a strong leader. When the group is challenged by another tribe, members fight enthusiastically to defend their territory, to get food, and to protect and keep their women. ( In his book "The Animal Within Us", Dr. Jay D. Glass, a double Ph.D. in neurobiology and psychology, calls these our "biobehavioral imperatives".) Those whose genes were not up for this kind of life did not survive or propagate, so these insticts are in the genes of all who survived, and that's every one of us here now, whether we have had individual occasion to explicitly recognize it or not. For me, these instincts were first stirred in my early teenage years reading the newspapers about the heroic Finns in 1939 defending on skis their country against the assault of heavy Russian tanks. Count me in! Iraq challenges no biobehavioral imperatives. Thus no enthusiasm. Count me out. Instead, I can sublimate my now aging imperatives, as most men do, by wildly and joyously rooting for my chosen tribe, The Red Sox, in their endless death struggle with their enemy, the Yankees.

\*\*\*\*\*\*\*\*\*\*\*\*\*\*

If they haven't had a truly bad time of it, older veterans—I am now one—may tend to glamorize war. Evolution favors memories which forget debilitating material and remember the energizing. Its hard to breed if you are badly haunted. Next, the healthy ego goes to work enhancing memories, padding its own obituary. Then audiences, large ones for movies or just a small group, seem always to like war stories and thus enable the glamorous telling. So it happens.

As a proven antidote to drifting too far this way I can personally recommend a visit, which will be tearful, to two powerful works of art; The Vietnam Wall and Glenna Goodacre's nearby bronze statue honoring the Vietnam Nurses.

# RANCHO DEL CABO DE TODOS SANTOS

In 1839 somewhere in the western wilderness of the United States my great great grandfather suddenly died and left his only traveling companion, a 9 year old son, an orphan. By the time he was 13 this boy, Charles Nordhoff, restless and resourceful, had gotten himself to Philadelphia where he signed on with Commodore Biddle and sailed to China on the 72 gun ship, The Columbia. After 3 years in the Navy, 3 as a whaler and 3 in the merchant fleet, he returned to Philadelphia and began his career as "the most significant newspaper reporter of the nineteenth century". He was the editor in turn of both of New York's major newspapers, explorer and astute evaluator of regional development, and best selling author of many books.

My mother, his granddaughter, often spoke of him in admiring terms as I was growing up. He had been born in Prussia and was an aristocrat, the name in Germany, she was wont to remark, having been Von Nordhoff. He was a fearless and courageous man, both physically and with his pen. I got a message which I liked. But he also championed liberal and idealistic causes, was not far from a pacifist, and harbored a lifelong interest in communal living. This was also appealing to me, but it was hard to integrate it all. He became my favorite ancestor, mysterious and alluring, and, despite some trouble that he has caused me, still is.

In 1875, in the midst of a busy editor's life, he set out on a long trip with his daughter Elsie and visited every communitarian group in the entire country and then published "The Communistic Societies of the United States". ("Shakers, Economists, Eben-ezers or Amana, Inspirationists, Zoarites, Oneida Perfectionists, Icarians, Bethel, Aurora, and other Communes.") This work became the reference book on this subject for both scholars and intellectual hippies and has been reprinted many times, even now, more than a 100 years after its first appearance. I have been fascinated by his summary at the book's end. After giving a perceptive analysis of why communal living fails he turns positive and says, "it gives independence and inculcates prudence and frugality. It demands self-sacrifice, and restrains selfishness and greed; and thus increases the happiness which comes from the moral side of human nature. Finally, it relieves the individual's life from a great mass of carking cares, from the necessity of over severe and exhausting toil, from the dread of misfortune or exposure in old age." He then quotes Luke's description of the primitive Christian church: "And all that believed were together, and had all things in common; and sold their possessions; and parted them to all men as every man had need". Then Charles Nordhoff writes, "These words have had a singular power over men in all ages since they were written." I surmise that these words had a singular power over my great grandfather and may help explain his 1887 last great venture, the only one he never wrote about, The Ranch of the Cape of All Saints.

On the west coast of North America there are not many narrow points of land that project far out into the Pacific Ocean. The Cape of All Saints, also known as Punta Banda, is one of them. About a four hour drive south of Los Angeles, two hours south of San Diego, this promontory thrusts its cactus and brush covered rocky spine out into the Pacific where that ocean's great rollers roar in against it day and night from a distance almost as great as any reach on earth. These waves tell you this about themselves just by the sound they make crashing against the red and brown headland rocks or in plunging into the small, cupped, sandy beaches hidden in between. The strength and beauty of this crashing of rock and surf is too overpowering to enjoy in any fashion other than to observe in awe. We are too small to receive in any way the caress of these waves, too inconsequential to be allowed even the least bit of help should we need it in a careless moment. Beauty and death are here together.

In dramatic contrast there lies to the north of Punta Banda a long sandy beach which runs for 12 miles in a great inward arc to the Mexican town of Ensenada. Behind the beach is an estero, or bay, of calm water for small boats , sea turtles, and myriad birds. Southward from the point the rocky coast leads on for about 18 miles, completely protected from access even now by a range of mountains too steep for roads. Between the mountains and the sea are great valleys and hillsides allowing only the most determined men on horseback and toughest cattle to penetrate the dense, wiry brush covering a land alive with rattlesnakes.

Here lies our family's Mexican ranch, purchased by Charles Nordhoff in 1887, The Ranch of the Cape of All Saints, 40,000 acres, 20 miles of Pacific coastline, and at the Northern boundary the central Ranch headquarters and buildings, called Ramahal, all having enticed and captured for many years four generations of Nordhoff men in powerful but unrewarding love affairs.

In 1952, probably because of my parent's wisdom, I knew practically nothing about this ranch, its history, its size, or even its location. But on a snowy night in January, on hill 854 in Korea, a runner from battalion headquarters delivered a telegram to me. My Grandmother Nordhoff had died. The telegram was from her daughter, my Aunt Mary, acting as estate executor in Santa Barbara. The telegram—I still have it—said, "YOU INHERIT RAMAHAL RANCH FORTY THOUSAND ACRES BACK TAXES AND CITIZENSHIP INVOLVED ADVISE WHEN POSSIBLE" My parents, back in suburban Connecticut, had they known of this telegram from beloved but nicely nutty Aunt Mary would probably have said, "Oh, God."

My head spun. I had no idea what this telegram meant for me, or was going to mean. Read it again for yourself and imagine how a 25 year old adventuresome young man would feel and dream on receiving it. It took a meeting with a lawyer from Division Headquarters to tell me I did not need to leave immediately, and then to help me figure out what to ADVISE. Essentially I responded with, "Sorry, I'm busy now, I'll take care of this when I get back home unless time is somehow of the essence."

It turned out that time was not of the essence, and had not been for a great while, but I did not know that. I was excited because I had learned to love Mexico in the summer of 1950 when climbing volcanoes there, because I spoke Spanish (Castilian), and chiefly because 40,000 acres of land, under any circumstances, clearly made me a millionaire. Anticipation of that happy state kept me at least a foot off the ground for a long time.

With my tour of duty in Korea over in the fall of '52 and now back in the Marine Corps' Camp Pendleton near San Diego, I bought an old Chevy and headed for the Ranch. Go to Ensenada, then 17 miles south, on the only road, (which leads an unpaved 800 miles further south to San Jose del Cabo at the tip of the Baja Peninsula), to the government check point on the highway. Talk to them, show respect, be prepared to find a dignified way to leave some pesos with them, and they will let you through and also tell you where your ranch is. I did, and with the old Chevy groaning up the rutted dirt hillside road I got to the ranch. I entered the deserted, large, main hall of my great grandfather's still strongly standing 60 year old masonry Ranch House, Ramahal. The glass was still in the big front windows and I saw below the uninhabited beach and estero heading to the North, Punta Banda to the west thrusting into the waves, and to the South the rampart of mountain protecting the main acreage of the Ranch. There was a large stone fireplace at each end of the long room. Feeling already that I belonged in this place, I walked the length of the room and stood in a door at the far end. Through it I saw an an aged Mexican woman standing in the servant's quarters. She gestured to me to come see what she was pointing at just outside a back door. A giant old fig tree with many ripened figs. Again with no words but only a gesture of her hands she said, "Please have one." I picked and put in my mouth a sun warmed fig. I had never eaten a fresh fig before. This was the moment, eating a sun-warmed fig from a tree probably planted by my great grandfather, at the invitation of this smiling grandmother, that I knew, really knew, what I wanted to do. And it most evidently wasn't going to be a job in an Insurance Company in Hartford, Connecticut. I would stay here, somehow.

My quickly developing dreams were for reestablishing a working cattle ranch with partners who had money to improve the land properly, or for creating a large seaside resort with riding, fishing and hunting sports. Should I fail with these goals I would just gather together some friends to join me in living here in a survivalist-hippie mode as best we could. A commune, perhaps. Having so far in life majored in philosophy, mountain climbing, and the Marine Corps, I was completely ignorant of how one proceeded to form companies or partnerships, sell stock and raise money. But I knew I needed a lawyer first. My Aunt Mary's lawyer said get the best one I could find in Ensenada. My Marine Corps savings would pay for that.

So wearing my uniform—I was still on active duty for several further months—I visited Ensenada, city of fishermen, bars, and ladies of the night, and with luck, before spending all my money on seaside entertainment, I found Alejandro La Madrid, Abogado (lawyer). He was about 35, had a small squared-away office, spoke some English, and seemed both serious and pleasant. For an estimated fee of $500 he would research the title, see about back taxes, and advise me about how I should proceed to perfect my title and develop the property. There would be difficulties, he said, not the least that Mexican law now disallowed a US citizen from owning land within either 60 miles of the sea or 100 miles of the border. The Ranch was both.

La Madrid told me it would take quite some time before he would be able to give me a full report. But this was all right because I now had to start looking for friends with money. Since I had no firm vision, no business plan, no cost estimates, and no shares to offer, my approach would be just to invite down to the ranch what friends and relatives I had or could find and let the place and my enthusiasm for it do the selling.

The first was Jim Fly, a fellow Marine officer, of British background, with money. His father was then head of the Federal Communications Commission. Both of us being young, strong, and adventurous, on our first trip we decided to swim in one of the small secret beaches out on the point. We slid, tumbled, and laughed down to the steep walled beach. As we stood in momentary delight on the drenched coarse sand, the first wave spotted us, rushed in on us, and we darn near didn't make it back up the slope before it caught us. We concluded the spot would be good for pictures on our Resort Brochure but we would have to find a gentler place to actually offer for guest swimming. As it turned out, for Jim the absence of any female guests there at the ranch right then was the more serious negative than dangerous waves.

Denny Fox, about whom I have written in "First Ascent with Denny Fox", was going to inherit The Vulcan Iron Works in Denver some day and he was one of my best friends. We visited the Ranch on the way to mountain climbing further down in Baja. Denny, though he liked mountain climbing, was simply not interested in anything to do with water, waves, oceans, or sandy beaches. He was a desert man and there was no desert here, and Beowulf, his other love, had never visited the place. His disinterest was totally evident in his expressions. We didn't need to discuss it. He went on to spend his professor's literary life very successfully at The University of Toronto.

While stationed at Camp Pendleton I often visited my Aunt Laura Nordhoff now living in La Jolla and a very good friend. She was a candidate with money herself. On his death she had inherited Charles Bernard Nordhoff's (Charles Nordhoff's grandson) rights to "Mutiny on The Bounty" and his other books. But more importantly she introduced me to some of the upper end of La Jolla and Santa Barbara society. Most vividly, I remember taking a pleasant, but overweight and overdressed young woman down to the ranch at her families strong urging. Their house on the hill overlooking La Jolla was then the biggest, best and most modern in that well-to-do town. I gained the impression from her father that if I would show serious interest in his daughter I might become well financed. He liked both Yale and the Marine Corps. He owned, I believe, The Grolier Encyclopedia Company. Can't remember the name. I have the feeling that his daughter was undoubtedly a good gal underneath. She wore a fulsome dirndl skirt I still remember. Oh, Fate! What would have happened had she weighed less, and had the accident of our chemistry been right? I still occasionally spend time building the dream.

Laura also introduced me to an anthropologist in Santa Barbara called Charris Crockett who had written a wonderful book, "The House in the Rain Forest", and she had known my Uncle Charles in Tahiti. She also lived in a big house on a hill, Montecito, overlooking the ocean. At breakfast time, after my first night there, the maid brought a tray into my bedroom. Along with coffee, orange juice and all the other essentials, there was a small glass of clear cold liquid. I thus discovered vodka years before it became popular and I stayed for quite a few more nights, and breakfasts.

Charris and Laura had a particularly good and well to do friend in Santa Barbara, an English man, named Teddy Baring-

Gould, of the hymn writing and financial family. He was 25 years older than I and had a wife and three kids, but we soon became very close friends almost as though we were the same age. He had a four wheel drive jeep, so useful in Mexico, and a daughter in college with the name of Sheena Marion Baring-Gould. Being me, I immediately fell in love with and coveted his jeep, but shortly thereafter his daughter as well. No friend could have been better than Teddy; he trusted me with both his treasures.

So with this group at the center I was meeting people who potentially had the money I needed, and even when sober they showed my dreams for the ranch a lot of interest and enthusiasm. They were not hippies, however, but that, after all, was only my fall back position.

We made several great safaris down to the ranch, camping out around a sage fire in the evening and spending the days exploring Ramahal, where even the library of my grandfather Walter Nordhoff was mostly intact after 30 years or so. We learned from the current residents and other locals that the house had been only periodically occupied by "squatters" and that for the most part they had been families that had worked on the ranch for previous Nordhoffs. The name meant a great deal to them. They were excited at the thought that we might be coming back. But for most locals Ramahal had been too remote and isolated and too high and dry above the valley floor to make farming and family life easy. So it was usually empty and, reflecting favorably on the community, had not been vandalized.

We ventured out onto precipitous and wild Punta Banda and we attempted to drive the jeep south into the interior of the ranch land. In this latter and important effort we were very unsuccessful because we could find no roads or even trails and the brush and cactus were too dense to allow any passage. A local Mexican guide was equally ineffective. The best he could show us was a beautiful long triple alley of eucalyptus trees planted by

Charles Nordhoff in one of the few flat places not far from Ramahal and still growing. They are such an outstanding sight in the otherwise scrubby brush verdure that to this day Mexican maps identify the place as "Las Arboles". These maps also show the place on Punta Banda known as "La Buffadora", or blow hole, where the waves push water into a rock crack and upward through a bore hole 60 or 70 feet high into the air.

Joining us on one trip was an older friend of the family who had visited the ranch in earlier days with my Uncle Charles when he had been actively interested in it. From this man I got the idea that establishing some sort of communal living might have been my great grandfather's original vision. The seed for this notion, communal living, was probably planted in me even earlier during the 1940s when I often visited my Great Aunt Elsie, Charles's daughter, at her farm in New Hampshire (where Sarah and I lived much later). Though she never spoke about the ranch, she idolized her father, became a member of the communist party, brought poor black women from Boston to live at the farm and berated me severely when I went off to Yale where I would meet only rich capitalists. Just the people I was now anxiously looking for.

So while waiting for lawyer La Madrid to finish his lengthy work, and while waiting for a large check to gently descend from the hands of one of my new friends, which was also taking longer than I thought it should, I was nonetheless having a very good time. Southern California can be great and I was getting my chance with it. Some peak moments were: being invited by Frank Lloyd Wright's son to cocktails and discussing architecture, attending my cousin Peter Morrison's million dollar Los Angeles wedding as his best man in my Marine Corps Dress Blues, being picked up hitchhiking by some wild young actors and actresses in their giant top down Cadillac convertible and being asked to join them at their afternoon Hollywood shoot. And all the time I was falling in love with Marion!

But my inability to get to the interior of the ranch, the very large area where my grandfather Walter had reportedly established herds of cattle, was a continuing worry. I needed to know what this terrain was like. Would it support cattle now? Was it attractive looking? Would one want to be there as either a resort guest or as a place to live?

Shortly before La Madrid was to give me his work, a uniquely valuable opportunity to penetrate this wilderness and answer these questions turned up. Three members of the Yale Mountaineering Club were in Southern California. Dick Merritt, Dave Crowell, and Zach Stewart. From first ascents in Alaska to winter mountaineering in the Adirondacks they had all been on tougher expeditions than a mere brushy stroll through the interior of Rancho del Cabo de Todos Santos. To make it fun, we would approach by climbing over the Eastern protective mountain range, with tallest peaks at about 3000 ft elevation, and then we would drop down into the western seaside valleys below. My anticipation of seeing what vast landscapes I owned was great, and my friends shared this with me.

But it was not to be. It took us all our strength, all our water, and all our enthusiasm to climb the 2000 or 3000 feet and arrive only after dark at the summit ridge line. It wasn't because we had Dick Merritt's wife with us. She was as good as any of us. None of us could move up through the dense and ferociously prickly head-high brush and cactus, past the tarantulas, scorpions, and rattlesnakes, at more that the slowest snails pace. Or more accurately, a millipedes pace, of which there were many ugly looking ones. We spent the night on the ridge, got a few wonderful glimpses of the Pacific under the moon, and slept a bit. The sun rose early and was immediately hot.

The previous day's climb had not really been mountaineering, and had not been at all fun. We studied the west side valleys which looked to be covered in exactly the same kind of cactus and brush as that we had come up through. We saw no grasslands, no level plains, no green trees, and above all no evidence of streams or water of any sort. So we decided not to go down into the Ranch interior. Even I, with so much at stake, was reconciled to turning back. I would get a better local guide and make another approach along sea level. There were 40 or 50 thousand acres there which would be mine and I wanted to stand on them and wanted to enjoy seeing them up close. My land. My own part of this good earth. It is such a warm, exciting feeling, much like love.

One could argue that my enthusiasm should perhaps by now have waned a bit, but when shortly after this trip the message came that LaMadrid was ready for me my heart raced, I put on my uniform again (I had stayed in the Reserve), and I whipped down that great old road from Tijuana to Ensenada. For an inexperienced young man with no money learning what he can and cannot do in this world with such opportunities as were before me, and how money can be raised to do them, is very serious learning. I, for one, could not have learned from books, would not have believed senior advice, nor could I have accepted the truth in any shorter time than it finally took. I had to learn my own way, through adventure, hard but exciting, slow but ultimately fully convincing and always fun.

LaMadrid's office looked just a bit more outfitted than I remembered. There were two comfortable chairs by a low table, and were there now flowers? He suggested we sit down, asked me how the drive down had been, and then suggested we have some coffee. He got up and tapped on the interior door of the office and said in a low voice to an occupant, "Listo, ahora", meaning "ready, now". Almost immediately a very attractive young Mexican woman, perhaps not yet 20, brought in a tray of coffee and pastry and placed it on the table. As she bent over to arrange things, he looked at me smilingly and said, "My daughter, Margarita. She helps me today."

Not yet having had any experience with lawyers, their offices or their help, I was nonetheless favorably impressed and felt surer than ever that I had chosen well in LaMadrid. He began his report to me with the subject of back taxes. The most important point was that my grandfather Walter Nordhoff was the last to have paid any taxes at all. The records showed that no one else had ever paid any. No town or county had ever moved to take possession for lack of tax payments. This was a wonderful start, and LaMadrid smiled with me. Next he talked about the *escritura*. I finally figured out it was the title, and he said something to the effect that the chain of ownership was uninterrupted and in good shape. But he also said something about titles granted during the days of President Porfirio Diaz not now being very strong. Both my great grandfather and my grandfather had been acquaintances, if not friends, of Diaz. Sometime after the uniquely long and stable Diaz era ended around 1910-11 a "return the land to the peasants" movement started and communal grants of old hacienda properties were made to the peasants and were called *Ejidos*. There were no *Ejidos* on my property now, but theoretically there might be in the future. It was, (and still is) an unclear and confusing issue. We left the subject since it was not a currently pressing obstacle.

From the beginning I had been most worried about the simpler problem of the land coming within 100 miles of the border and 60 miles of the sea. LaMadrid agreed this was a major issue. Becoming a little more formal and authoritative he said that there were three legal solutions which he had presented for other US landowners in the region. He explained at some length how he would create a bank trust for me, which I also did not really understand, or, alternatively, he would form a company to own the property which company would have 51% of the stock held by Mexicans. He did not mention who these Mexicans might be and how much they might be asked to pay for their 51% share, but he passed on so quickly to the next and last option that I concluded he did not favor the earlier ones. I could see and sense a happy pride developing in my lawyer, an excitement and enthusiasm for the proposal he was about to present me, my final option. His enthusiasm carried me with him. He rose from his chair, leaving me in expectant hope, and walked over to the door the coffee had come from and knocked on it again as he had before.

She must have been standing right there behind the door waiting for the knock. Given what was about to happen to this young woman, his daughter, she carried off the scene and the moments to come with the equanimity, grace, and allure of a country princess. With an intense but smiling face Alejandro LaMadrid, Abogado, said to me, his client, "Senor, Patron, I advise you with certainty that the simplest way to hold strongly the possession of your ancestor's great ranch is to take for you a Mexican wife. Here is my daughter, Margarita, whom you have already met. She would be happy to fulfill these needs for you and would make a very good family."

Wiped out as I was, flustered, speechless, and embarrassed, I still love Mexico and my Abogado. What a way to do business. Complete service. I survived the moment, gave something like the classic, "I'll have to think hard about your most generous offer", and managed not to hurt anyone's feelings. Attesting to the excellence of my Andover education, even the exactly right phrase for Margarita assembled itself on my lips to say to her as she retired once again, with an honest smile, to the coffee room. "Me gusto mucho en conocerlo." (Page 27, first year Spanish book.) "It pleases me much to know you."

As for the ending of this story—the events of 3 or 4 months culminating in this meeting—sadly I never saw Margarita again, because, and perhaps also sadly, I did not have the courage or dream power to follow her father's hopes, marry her, and move immediately to the ranch. What I see and know today is that we would most probably have been poor by United States standards but perhaps rich by local Mexican standards, and we would never have been hungry. We would have farmed, fished, swum in the bay, hiked in the hills and raised a few burros. I would have joined a large LaMadrid family, and in the surrounding region I would have become affectionately known as "Nuestro Patron Sin Dinero" (our Patron without money). Margarita would be the adored mother of 12, enough to form our own *Ejido* and lay claim to Ramahal in the modern way should that have become necessary. The vast expanse of the remote, dry, rugged, but beautiful 50,000 seaside acres of El Rancho del Cabo de Todos Santos, which was to have made me a millionaire, would remain, just as it has been in actuality to this day, undeveloped and endlessly waiting for God,—to Whom Margarita and I would have prayed,—to bless it with bountiful rains.

*******************

Epilogue

But my failure to marry Margarita and grasp in hand this risky, romantic, Mexican life, one that also could perhaps even have developed into the idealized commune, was not really just a failure of my courage. In further conversations with LaMadrid that morning the picture developed that yes, I could live at Ramahal, and perhaps very happily. The Mexicans and their law would welcome me, especially while I was drilling new and much needed water wells, clearing land for agriculture, and making other improvements even on a small scale, but all land except that of the ranch house itself could rather easily be taken away from me if the place got in any way noticeably valuable, or if development moved down the bay from Ensenada. The poor people's right to land through the *Ejido* process was fundamental Mexican law, and there was even occasional talk of making Punta Banda a provincial or national park. LaMadrid emphasized all these points several times, anxious that I understood.

214

Thus it became clear that one of my main goals, to create value, would be self defeating. I think that that realization was what finally cut me down. On the other hand, Margarita's father, my abogado, clearly would have liked to see me try to reinvigorate the ranch, with his and his daughter's help, and I do not hold it against him that it was possibly because he thought I had more money than the none I thus far did have. He was a truly good, honest, and level advisor and time has proven that he was also wise. You shall see. And he offered complete service.

********

In the fifty-three years since 1953 when I stood gazing seaward from Ramahal's front porch and said goodbye to the dream with a tearing in my heart, as my Great Grandfather Charles had done in 1891, and his son Walter had done around 1920, I have learned quite a few more bits of relevant and interesting information about the ranch. The last item with a date as recent as April 2006.

But first I must give my father credit for research he did around 1960 about rainfall in Baja California. The figures were hard to come by. But he concluded that the ten or fifteen years preceding Charles Nordhoff's original purchase of the ranch had been unusually wet and it had been essentially dry ever since.

This fact can explain why Nordhoff, who had very successfully founded the towns of Alpine, New Jersey, and Ojai, California (both originally called Nordhoff until the elimination of German names) selected a place in Baja California that would not thrive. It had been wet and green when he got there. But it didn't last.

According to family history I learned from my mother shortly before she died, Charles and Walter had had a severe argument in 1891 about how to manage the even then modest water supply of the ranch. The older man apparently lost the fight. He left unhappy and never returned. (Went to Hawaii to help the native Queen fight expropriation by the US.)

Essentially alone at the ranch, Walter continued off and on for 30 years using his wife's Philadelphia Quaker inheritance in futile attempts to grow farm crops and raise beef cattle. I have discovered and read his sparse ranch journals and they show small production and much discouragement. A July 1903 entry says, only, "Received news today of father's death in San Francisco. No rain." His family, including my mother, were there but only occasionally.

A valuable fruit of another sort, however, was slowly growing and did mature at Ramahal. Walter learned to understand and deeply love Mexican culture and history and wrote six novels about it. The two he published both became **Book Of The Month Club** selections one of which, "The Journey of the Flame", is republished regularly. (He wrote under the pen name *Antonio de Fierro Blanco* in order not to trade on his own son Charles's then flowering reputation.) His sister, my previously mentioned Great Aunt Elsie, once visited the ranch and got a story published in **Harpers**. It was about an easterner suffering badly out west on a ranch as she listened all night to the cattle lowing in thirst and dying by day.

I have already mentioned that I discovered and read "Communistic Societies of the United States" sometime after settling down in Hartford, Connecticut. While working after hours in the evenings at my job with The Hartford Steam Boiler Inspection and Insurance Company (yes, I succumbed) I had become friends with our elderly night watchman who owned and ran a small used book store in town. With my support he began a plan to buy me a copy of every book written by Charles Nordhoff. My family had only a very few. The second book he brought me was a surprise. No family member had ever mentioned it. Here is the title page:

PENINSULAR CALIFORNIA
some account of
The Climate, Soil, Productions, and
Present Condition Chiefly of
the Northern Half of
LOWER CALIFORNIA
by
CHARLES NORDHOFF
author of
"California: for Health, Pleasure, and Residence"
"God and the Future Life"
"Politics for Young Americans"
"Cape Cod and all Along the Shore"
"Communistic Societies of the United States"
etc.
NEW YORK
Harper and Brothers, Franklin Square
1888

Though I had thoroughly abandoned all dreams of living in the Baja, I devoured this book with an interest and excitement which revealed that a few strands of the ranch's rusty barbed wire still ensnared my blue jeans—so many years later, and 3000 miles away!

It is an elegant leather bound volume and its contents are just as they are listed on the title page. There are photos of fruit trees and farmers. The descriptions of fertile, unoccupied, and well watered farmland sound glorious, but excessively so. Soon, on rereading it, the book's true nature began to dawn on me. I have concluded that Charles Nordhoff wrote the book with a mission, to promote the settlement of land, and sell real estate, in northern Baja California. And the real estate Company in charge was named in the book and was headquartered no further away than the town in which I was now reading the book, Hartford Conn. Doing further research I found I knew the names of the old Hartford men that owned and ran the Company! What sort of deal did they have with my great grandfather? An enjoyable coincidence and mystery!

Historically the development of Mexico and most particularly Baja California had lagged very far behind the United States, thus in 1883 President Diaz decided to privatize and outsource the work of colonizing the remoter provinces. **The Mexican International Company of Hartford, Connecticut** was granted the absolutely amazing exclusive and complete concession to to sell all the land in northern Baja California between the Latitudes 28 and 32.42 degrees (the border with the US). This was a band of land from the Pacific Ocean to the Gulf of Mexico and about 300 miles from north to south. Approximately 16,000,000 acres! They had to survey it and pay some money, but the real challenge given to them by the Mexican government was to bring in and get established 2000 colonizing families in the ten years between 1887 and 1897 or they would lose the land that had not been settled. Charles Nordhoff's exuberant book describes all this, and starts with the statement that in 1887 he selected and bought a "small" tract of land on and near the bay of Todos Santos. This much is pretty clear and certain.

But a surmise I entertain, and one that leads me to think a little differently about my great grandfather, is that the Hartford men had noticed the very great success of Nordhoff's 1872 book extolling the virtues of settlement in California proper and made a deal with him. They would get a book helping to bring the needed 2000 settlers to Baja, and Nordhoff would get a ranch,—and one with 20 miles of coastline! I do not know if they faired any better with getting their settlers than he did with de-

veloping his ranch. I wonder if they now have any 5th generation descendants still enjoying their side of the deal?

I have made two visits to the ranch since learning this history.
In 1982 Sarah and I visited and found Ramahal occupied by a
British actress, Victoria Faust. Curiously, she was quite knowledgeable about the Nordhoffs and, rather improbably, said she
had specifically sought out and somehow acquired the ranch as a
place to retire. In order to secure her possession she had married
an important Mexican, the local highway construction superin-
tendent. The husband had since died but they'd had a daughter.

Thumb tacked to the cracked and peeling plaster walls of
Ramahal were old and ragged newspaper pictures of Victoria
with British Royalty, but also pictures of my Uncle Charles
Nordhoff and reviews of his books. The one couch and one
chair in the once grand living room were worn and dirty from
having served as beds for the many dogs who shared her home. I
was sad to find old hypodermic needles in the front yard.

But at sunset, with birds flying in and out of large holes in the
eaves, Victoria sat down at the grand, hand carved, magnificent
old piano, miraculously still well tuned, and with eyes closed,
swaying on the bench, played with great skill and emotion several classical compositions. Still full of rich power this aged per-
former transported Sarah and me in awe into the mystical world
of departed ancestors along with their generations of Mexican
helpers, their dogs, and all their dreams.

In 2002 my two oldest sons, Mike and James, visited
Ramahal with me. Victoria was dead and her daughter gone, but
her grandson son, Carlos, welcomed us and knew who we were.
He was very pleasant but also very poor and the place showed it.
He and Mike, who sat on the old piano bench, spent much time
talking and I saw the next generation start to get lost in the old
dream and maybe get taken in and captured.

Ramahal still stood alone at the top end of the dirt road but
there were now houses almost all the way up to it. Carlos had

dreams, but one in particular was the strongest. In pursuit of it he and his local friends spent most of their time in the hills behind the house digging for that which my great grand father had buried at Ramahal, a large cache of gold. Surely I must know where it was? Would I show him?

There were now several paved roads and one led down to an extensive beach front development. There were some very elegant and apparently well maintained houses, but all seemed unoccupied. There were many more buildings whose construction had stopped about half way through. Boards and even rusty tools still lay around. Most common were completed houses with broken windows, doors swinging in the pacific breeze, and graffiti on the white bright sunlit walls.

Understandable explanations of this ghostly and puzzling scene were not forthcoming from the locals. I had to wait until the April 18th 2006 **Wall Street Journal:**

"Conflicts over title aren't uncommon in Mexico. In the year 2000, some 200 American homeowners were evicted from their luxury development on the Baja coast, after a court ruled against the developer in a convoluted title dispute." Just what LaMadrid had accurately foreseen 50 years earlier.

I should not, but nonetheless I do like to think there may be future Nordhoff chapters in the story of the Rancho del Cabo de Todos Santos. There is no real reason why there couldn't be. Any descendant could drive down the 17 miles south of Ensenada, buy out the current residents of Ramahal for a very few thousand dollars, and move in. But he had better marry a Mexican.